SHREWSBURY SCHOOL LIBRARY

15 52

INTUS SI RECTE NE LABORE

Critical Guides to French Texts

43 Aragon: The Resistance Poems

Critical Guides to French Texts

EDITED BY ROGER LITTLE, WOLFGANG VAN EMDEN, DAVID WILLIAMS

ARAGON

The Resistance Poems
(*Le Crève-cœur, Les Yeux d'Elsa*
and *La Diane française*)

M. Adereth

Senior Lecturer
University of Lancaster

Grant & Cutler Ltd
1985

© Grant & Cutler Ltd
1985
ISBN 0 7293 0209 1

I.S.B.N. 84-599-0398-2

DEPÓSITO LEGAL: V. 286 - 1985

Printed in Spain by
Artes Gráficas Soler, S.A., Valencia
for
GRANT & CUTLER LTD
11 BUCKINGHAM STREET, LONDON W.C.2

Contents

Preface   7

1. Circumstances   9

2. Structure   14

3. Themes   22

4. Poetic Technique   53

5. Impact   71

Select Bibliography   78

Acknowledgements

May I offer my sincere thanks to Professor Roger Little, one of the editors of the series, for his patience and most helpful suggestions; to Professor Wolfgang van Emden, another editor and a personal friend, who read my original text with great care and suggested many felicitous alterations; to Dr Keith Wren, my friend and colleague, who helped me with many valuable comments; and to Dr Susan Taylor-Horrex, another good friend and colleague, whose assistance and encouragement proved invaluable.

Preface

The three collections of poems which are discussed in this study were written by Aragon during the Second World War. They are the most important of his 'Resistance poems', so called because they were largely meant as contributions to France's many-sided Resistance struggle (economic, political, military and intellectual) against her Nazi occupiers. In all three cases, my references are to the most readily available edition, viz. Gallimard, Collection Poésie, 1980, for *Le Crève-cœur*; Seghers, 1971, for *Les Yeux d'Elsa*; and Seghers, 1971, for *La Diane française*. Many of the poems in these collections had been known in France and abroad well before their appearance in book form, as they had been printed individually either in newspapers and periodicals or by the underground Resistance press. References to the select bibliography at the end of this study are by number in italics followed by page numbers (e.g. *20*, p.92).

Finally, a personal reminiscence. I first became acquainted with Aragon's work through an English edition of *Le Crève-cœur* and *Les Yeux d'Elsa*, and I still remember how much I agreed with Cyril Connolly who wrote in the introduction that through Aragon, 'England (had) received its first war-poet' because he had made 'music out of the war' and had been able 'to release by his craft the emotions of millions' (*22*, pp.7-8). It is of course impossible that the same emotion will be felt by modern, younger readers, whether British or French, but many might find in Aragon's Resistance poems an echo of a bygone era which had its own grandeur and appeal.

Note on abbreviations used

As three different collections of poems are discussed, the following abbreviations have been used when giving page references:

> *CC* for *Le Crève-cœur*
> *YE* for *Les Yeux d'Elsa*
> *DF* for *La Diane française*

1. Circumstances

In order fully to understand Aragon's wartime poems, it is useful to have some knowledge of the historical and biographical background against which they were written, not only because of the many allusions to political and personal events which these poems contain, but also because their author believes with Goethe that all poems are 'poèmes de circonstance'. In his case, at any rate, this is certainly true.

In France, the Second World War was preceded by the Popular Front experiment, which was a left-wing alliance against fascism at home and abroad. After ruling the country for about two years, the alliance collapsed in 1938. It received a final death blow in August 1939, because the signing of the Soviet-German non-aggression pact further sharpened the divisions among the members of the alliance. The Communists, while continuing to demand resistance to Hitler, supported the pact as a defensive measure on the USSR's part, whereas their Socialist and Radical ex-partners roundly condemned it as treason. The government banned the Communist daily, *L'Humanité*, on 26 August 1939 and outlawed the party itself a month later. Many Communists and Communist sympathisers were arrested and jailed. Veiled references to these facts may be found in Aragon's poems in *Le Crève-cœur*, as for example, the mention in the opening piece, 'Vingt ans après', of thousands of prisoners in their cells: ostensibly, this was a description of the French soldiers who, like Aragon, were 'prisoners' in their barracks, but it also alluded to the poet's political friends who had been deprived of their freedom.

The first few months of the war were characterised by an almost complete lack of military operations, as the British and French armies simply waited for the Germans to attack. This bewildered so many people that the phrase, *la drôle de guerre*, was coined. Clandestine Communist propaganda laboured the point that the western powers did not really want to fight Hitler, because they hoped that he would eventually realise that his only enemy was Russia. As a Communist, Aragon naturally endorsed his party's condemnation of the phoney war, but he also spoke for many Frenchmen when he complained in his early verse of being kept idle for no apparent purpose. On 10 May 1940, the Germans attacked the Low Countries, and, a few days later, they invaded France. They met with little organised resistance, and on 14 June, they entered Paris, which surrendered without a fight. The new leader of France, Marshal Pétain, agreed to an armistice, which split the country into an occupied northern zone and a nominally free zone in the south. The Pétain government left the capital and established its headquarters at Vichy, soon embarking upon a policy of co-operation with the occupiers and condoning the Germans' worst excesses, including the institution in February 1943 of the S.T.O. (*Service du Travail Obligatoire*), a decree which ordered the compulsory deportation of French workers to Germany. Supporters of Vichy became known as 'collaborators'.

In the meantime, opposition to Vichy and the invaders had begun to take shape. At first, it was mostly a verbal opposition, but it quickly grew to embrace all forms of activity, strikes, sabotage, and above all guerilla warfare conducted by military groups, of which the most important was the *Francs-Tireurs et Partisans* (F.T.P.). The hiding places of these groups were known as *maquis*, a word which until then had been used to designate the bushes where Corsican bandits hid from the police. In the common fight against the Germans, members of the Resistance shed their political and ideological differences and a remarkable degree of unity was achieved. All the same, the movement was split into pro-Gaullist and pro-Communist trends, the supporters of de Gaulle being in favour of waiting for liberation by the Free French Forces (whose H.Q. was in London) and the Anglo-American armies, and the others advocating the liberation of one area of France after another by the local population and *maquis*. The Gaullists were nicknamed *attentistes* (people who wait and see) by their rivals, and many of Aragon's poems in *La Diane française* were open attacks on *attentiste* attitudes. Although the conflict was never fully resolved, *attentisme* eventually made way for militancy, and this culminated in the liberation of Paris by the Parisians themselves in August 1944.

If we now turn to Aragon himself, we should note that he was in his forties when the war broke out and had already led a fairly eventful literary and personal life. He began his career as a supporter of Dada, a trend which arose in 1916 and preached absolute revolt, and of surrealism, a movement which grew out of Dada and attempted to supplement revolt by the exploration of a higher reality (*sur-réalité*). It was claimed that this higher reality could be found in the sub-conscious and had to be conveyed by means of fresh, spontaneous writing, *l'écriture automatique*. The leading surrealists were Breton, Aragon and Eluard. In his personal life, Aragon went from one unhappy love affair to another until he met Elsa Triolet in November 1928. She was a Russian by birth but had left her native country in 1918 in order to follow her first husband to France. Elsa Triolet and Louis Aragon soon realised that they needed each other, and, despite a few ups and downs in the early years, they remained together until Elsa's death in 1970. It is difficult to sum up all that the poet owes to his wife, as there is hardly a book in verse or in prose in which he fails to mention his debt to her. In fact, such is his insistence that he is nothing but Elsa's 'shadow' and that his life really began the moment he met her that some critics have dismissed all his assertions as literary elegance rather than the expression of genuine feeling. Aragon's humility before Elsa is certainly unusual and at times embarrassing, but it is in keeping with his passion for the absolute and his rejection of half measures.

At the same time as Aragon was embarking upon a new personal adventure with Elsa Triolet, he was also in the process of making a break with his intellectual and ideological past. Although he had joined the Communist party in 1927, it was in the early thirties that he became a militant and brought his art and his politics together. This led him to part company with his surrealist friends. Most of them had joined the Communist party at the same time as he, but they soon fell foul of the party leadership and left. Aragon, on the other hand, wanted to become involved in 'the real world', as he called it, and to serve his cause both as a man and as an artist. He claimed, however, that this was not a betrayal of his youthful ideals, because the logic of surrealism demanded that one should go beyond it and discard its own dogmas, as for example, the 'dogma' of 'free verse' as the *only* expression of spontaneity, or the 'dogma' of a Chinese Wall between art and politics. Abandoning poetry for a while, Aragon started a series of novels, to which he gave the general title of *Le Monde réel*, and became a journalist, working first for the Communist daily, *L'Humanité*, and later taking over the editorship of another Communist daily, *Ce Soir*.

When the war broke out in September 1939, Aragon was called up. It was the first time he had been separated from Elsa and he felt the need to express his grief in poetry. Another factor which helped to revive his poetic inspiration was his wish to share with other French people his opposition to the phoney war, his anger against the June 1940 capitulation, and, eventually, his hatred of German occupation. His first poems were published individually in various newspapers and periodicals, but when, in 1941, Gallimard brought out a collection of them under the title of *Le Crève-cœur*, all copies were sold out in a few days. There had not been such a demand for poetry for a long time. And of course the demand actually increased after the Germans suppressed the book. During the last stages of the military campaign, Aragon was decorated for bravery, then escaped from Dunkirk to England (together with thousands of others), returned to France, was captured by the Germans, escaped after a few hours, and finally, he made his way to the southern zone, accompanied by Elsa. There, the couple wasted no time in trying to organise intellectual resistance against the Nazis. One of their closest collaborators was Pierre Seghers, who had edited *Poètes casqués* during the war. The magazine changed its name to *Poésie 40*, then to *Poésie 41* and so on, and it carried poems by many Resistance writers. They also had links with other periodicals, e.g. *Fontaine*, published in North Africa by Max-Pol Fouchet, and *Les Cahiers du Rhône*, published in neutral Switzerland by Albert Béguin.

In June 1941, Aragon and Elsa went to Paris in order to liaise with other Resistance writers, but, as they crossed the 'frontier' between the two zones at Tours, they were arrested and had to spend a few days in an internment camp (see the opening lines of 'Richard Cœur-de-Lion' in *YE*, p.73). Fortunately, their German captors had not heard of the poet's fame and they released the couple in July. On their return to the south, they continued to be active and live under assumed names, but they had to go into hiding after 11 November 1942, as, on that day, the Germans occupied the whole of the country and the Italians entered France. Until the middle of 1943, Aragon was able to publish his poems openly, although, in order to do so, he had to disguise his real thoughts and resort to hints and allusions. His confidence that the censors would be taken in whilst patriots would divine his meaning proved justified, and the three 'legal' collections, *Les Yeux d'Elsa* (1942), *Brocéliande* (1942), and *En français dans le texte* (1943), had the same success as their predecessor, *Le Crève-cœur*. However, the poems that followed had to be printed by the Resistance clandestine press. They included the 1943 collection, *Le Musée Grévin*, and the poems of *La Diane française*. All those who came into contact with Aragon during the Resistance years later paid tribute to his courage and dedication. For example, writing in *Our Time* in November 1944, Nancy Cunard described him as 'undefeatable by danger and fatigue, [...] the embodiment of all that France has been again and again in times of stress and danger in the defence of human liberty [...]'.

2. Structure

According to Malcolm Cowley, Aragon's wartime poetry 'became a month-by-month record of the struggle' (*23*, p.8) waged by himself and his contemporaries. Naturally, it would be idle to expect any one volume to have a unified structure, but each of them does have a kind of pattern or unity, not unlike the pattern which is revealed by the TV programme, 'This is Your Life'. Aragon's poems are the record of his life and that of his generation, and as such they reproduce the mood of the times which gave them birth. In 1940-41, that mood was essentially one of 'heartbreak', caused by France's national misfortune, and the poems of *Le Crève-cœur* artistically convey such a mood. In 1941-42, to the sense of tragedy was added one of defiance and hope, and, in Aragon's poems of the period, the combination of the two aspects was reflected in Elsa's eyes, so that *Les Yeux d'Elsa* was a fitting title for the next collection. Finally, in 1943-44, the French people's mood had become a fighting mood, and it was then, as the opening prose piece of *La Diane française* puts it, that reveille sounded throughout the land:

> Alors la diane française sonna.   (*DF*, p.13)

Let us now see how each of these moods is in fact illustrated in the relevant collection.

In *Le Crève-cœur*, Aragon's heartbreak has four main causes: separation from Elsa, the war, the character of the war, and the defeat. These aspects are inter-related because they are so many facets of the same agonising reality. The separation from Elsa is mentioned right at the beginning and is poignantly conveyed by the recurring theme of letters as the only form of contact between husband and wife (see the poems, 'Vingt ans après', 'J'attends sa lettre au crépuscule', 'Petite suite sans fil', and 'Les amants séparés'). The reason why Aragon and Elsa cannot be together is of course the war, the second cause of his heartbreak, and this time the recurring theme is that of twenty years, the mere twenty years which elapsed between the First and the Second World Wars (see the poems, 'Vingt ans après', 'Chant de la zone des étapes' and 'La Valse des vingt ans'). An additional war theme is found in 'Deux poèmes d'outre-tombe', one of them evoking the Trojan war and the suffering it caused, and the other, the 1936-39 Spanish Civil War, which, according to Aragon, had stirred genuine popular anti-fascism among the Republicans, in sharp contrast with the apathy which prevailed in France in 1939. This brings us to the third cause of Aragon's heartbreak, the fact that during the *drôle de guerre*, the French government had done little to instil a real desire to fight. As a result, people were bored and frustrated. For example, Aragon, stationed at Crouy-sur-Ourcq, found himself killing, not the enemy, but the weary hours which died painfully:

> Que les heures tuées
> Guerre à Crouy-sur-Ourcq
> Meurent mal [...]   (*CC*, p.14)

Another poem, 'Le Temps des mots croisés', is a more scathing attack on the phoney war, first because the poet dissociates himself from the government and its supporters by asserting that he is not 'one of theirs', and secondly because French rulers are made to look rather silly for having banned crossword puzzles in the press on the ground that they might contain coded messages. Finally, two poems allude to the abortive attempt to end the *drôle de guerre* in April 1940. The first one, 'Le Printemps', complains that no offensive took place in the spring, as had been hopefully expected, and the second one, 'Romance du temps qu'il fait', ironically suggests that the war having aborted, one can only talk of the weather.

The last nine poems of *Le Crève-cœur* were all written between July and October 1940 and they express the heartbreak caused by the loss of national independence. The best known of them, 'Les Lilas et les roses', owes its title to the two flowers

which symbolise the two stages of the May-June 1940 war, the
lilacs which greeted French troops in Belgium as the people
'smothered' them with flowers because they expected instant
Allied victory, and the roses which retreating French soldiers
and civilians found everywhere they went as they fled towards
the south of France. One of the last lines briefly mentions the
surrender of Paris, and its very brevity conveys a feeling of
poignancy:

> On nous a dit ce soir que Paris s'est rendu
>
> (*CC*, p.41)

Another poem describes the way in which civilians, fleeing from
the Germans, were stopped by 'barrages' of *gendarmes* and sent
back home. The title, 'Complainte pour l'orgue de la nouvelle
barbarie', contains an untranslatable pun, as *orgue de barbarie*
is the name given to a barrel organ, whilst *barbarie* by itself
means barbarism. The defiant refusal to accept German
occupation finds its first expression in the poem, 'Richard II
Quarante', in which each stanza ends with the reminder that the
poet remains 'king of his griefs', like Richard II in
Shakespeare's play.

  But *Le Crève-cœur*, despite its title, is not only about heartbreak; it also has a message of hope. The fact that Aragon wrote
it at all is a sign of hope, for a man who was literally heart-
broken would not have been able to speak of his distress in
verse. As André Labarthe rightly remarked, '*Le Crève-cœur*
vient d'où les cœurs ne crèvent pas' (*22*, p.6). We touch here
upon a crucial characteristic of all first-rate poetry, which is
what Keats called the poet's 'negative capability'. By this he did
not mean detachment or indifference, but the artist's power to
stand outside himself. It is true that only a deep emotion can be
at the origin of a poem which is more than a skilled piece of
craftsmanship, but the poem itself stands as proof that its
author has been able to transcend his emotion, to 'negate' it. As
Wordsworth wrote, poetry represents 'emotion recollected in
tranquillity'. The last two poems of *Le Crève-cœur* are mostly
poems of hope. In 'Les Croisés', which blends medieval and

modern history, it is the love of freedom which sustains Aragon's hope, and in 'Elsa je t'aime', it is his love for his wife.

In *Les Yeux d'Elsa* the general pattern is clear, because each poem illustrates one of the two aspects which are mirrored in Elsa's eyes — tragedy, on the one hand, and hope and defiance, on the other. The opening poem, which gives its title to the whole collection, sets the tone, and can be seen as the overture of an opera whose finale is the poet's hymn to his wife, the 'Cantique à Elsa'. Before this finale, Elsa seems to be in the background, but actually, she is the mainspring of Aragon's inspiration, and, even when she is not mentioned by name, her presence can be felt.

The poems which express tragedy can be divided into three categories. First, we have the laments of the four 'Nuits' and of the three 'Plaintes'. The former openly recall the poems of that name in which Alfred de Musset spoke of his sorrow, but with the exception of 'La Nuit de Mai', Aragon's 'Nights' have different titles, which makes it clear that his theme is not unrequited love but the grief of the militant patriot who witnessed the debacle of May 1940 ('La Nuit de Mai'), the Dunkirk panic ('La Nuit de Dunkerque'), the reduction of French people into exiles in their own country ('La Nuit d'exil') and the darkness which descended upon France when foreign troops occupied her soil ('La Nuit en plein midi'). The three 'Plaintes', although they take us back to the sixteenth century and the Middle Ages, are more concerned with the continuity between past and present misfortunes. The last one in particular, 'Plainte pour le grand descort de France' (in Old French, *descort* meant dissension and/or strife) obviously refers to modern France when it describes a country in which the image of love has been lost (*YE*, p.68). The fact that the poem was written in May brings back the memory of those who died in May 1940 and also of the members of the Paris Commune who were savagely executed in May 1871. Aragon alludes to the latter in the last three lines:

> Je n'oublierai jamais pour ses fleurs la muraille
> > Je n'oublierai jamais
> > Les morts du mois de Mai   (*YE*, p.69)

The 'muraille' is obviously the *Mur des Fédérés*, the wall where French left-wingers annually lay their wreaths, and Aragon later remarked that it was only the Vichy censors' ignorance and their lack of 'solide éducation surréaliste' (*DF*, p.89) which prevented them from understanding the allusion.

Another way of conveying a sense of tragedy is the bitter irony which pervades the two poems, 'Fêtes galantes', which exposes the senselessness and inhumanity of the new regime, and 'Les Folies-Giboulées', which deliberately makes use of the two meanings of the word 'temps': in the opening line it seems to describe the weather, but at the end it clearly means 'the times', for we are told of a 'temps' in which friends have turned into foes, black into white, what was forbidden into what is allowed, and the best has become the worst. The third category of tragic poems includes elegies, of which the most moving is probably the poem, 'C', with its recurring sound, *cé*, at the end of every line. The 'ponts de Cé' of the first line are the four Caesar bridges across which the Gauls retreated in 51 B.C. and the French army in June 1940.

The first poem expressing hope and defiance is 'Richard Cœur-de-Lion', which includes this open encouragement to Resistance fighters:

> Ils sont la force et nous sommes le nombre
> Vous qui souffrez nous nous reconnaissons
>
> (*YE*, p.74)

The three poems which follow, 'Pour un chant national', 'Contre la poésie pure', and 'Plus belle que les larmes', put forward an impassioned case for committed poetry in wartime. The last one was a reply to Aragon's former friend, Drieu la Rochelle, now turned 'collaborator'. The final poem of the collection is in six parts, of which the fourth one, 'Ce que dit Elsa', poetically reports Elsa Triolet's plea that the poet should use plainer language so that he should be understood by all those who have neither the time nor the opportunity to consult dictionaries and would therefore like to hear

> [...] des mots ordinaires
> Qu'ils se puissent tout bas répéter en songeant
>
> (*YE*, p.104)

The last collection of wartime poems, *La Diane française*, owes its unity to the fact that all the pieces are, in one way or another, calls for resistance. The poet makes his appeal in six different ways. First, he stresses that in 1943-44, the time for action is ripe and that *attentisme* is wrong. For example, the prose preface claims that resistance grew spontaneously as the French people became more confident of victory. The opening poem which is intended as a *Marseillaise* brought up to date ('Formez vos bataillons', *DF*, p.16), ends with a dismissal of the *attentiste* argument that the *maquisards* should wait for arms from abroad:

> Des armes où trouver des armes
> Il faut les prendre à l'ennemi   (*DF*, p.16)

The attack on *attentisme* becomes more pointed in the two poems, 'Le Drôle de printemps' and 'Chanson du Franc-Tireur', for both make a derogatory use of the verb *attendre*, the first one to ask impatiently, 'qu'attends-tu' (*DF*, p.24), and the second one to tell France that her sons have already chosen — not to wait:

> N'attends pas tes fils ont choisi   (*DF*, p.44)

Finally, in 'Les roses de Noël', the poet evokes the early Resistance fighters, and in 'Marche française', he asserts:

> Il faut libérer ce qu'on aime
> Soi-même soi-même soi-même   (*DF*, p.71)

A second way of calling for resistance is to extol the unity of all patriots, which Aragon does in a number of poems, especially in 'La Rose et le réséda', which is dedicated to four martyrs, two Catholics and two Communists, and relies for part of its appeal on the recurring lines:

> Celui qui croyait au ciel
> Celui qui n'y croyait pas   (*DF*, pp.19-20)

Thirdly, there are poems which praise the dignified heroism of the Resistance, either by recalling the martyrdom of individual fighters such as the Communist, Gabriel Péri (*DF*, pp.37-39 and 65-67), or by glorifying the Resistance as a whole, as in 'Gloire', or by singling out the heroism of such cities as Lyons, Strasbourg, and above all Paris, whose self-liberation is hailed in the penultimate poem of the collection.

Fourthly, Aragon exposes the cruelty of the enemy, who is forcibly deporting French workers to Germany ('Romance des quarante mille' and 'La Délaissée'), or is savagely killing defenceless children ('D'une petite fille massacrée'). Mussolini, Hitler's ally, is not spared, and in July 1943, the poet welcomes the news that the Italian dictator has fallen:

> C'est encore une fois Juillet dont les dents brillent
> C'est toujours en Juillet que grillent les Bastilles
>   (*DF*, p.55)

Fifthly, in the Resistance struggle, poets have a special part to play, and two poems are specifically addressed to them. In 'Six tapisseries inachevées', the tapestries stand for Resistance art. France is likened to a medieval Lady, and Aragon to Lancelot, the knight who is ready to save her:

> J'ai rencontré ma Dame au bord de l'eau
> Ma Dame est France et moi son Lancelot
>   (*DF*, p.17)[1]

The other poem, 'Je ne connais pas cet homme', reads like a

---

[1] In all editions of *La Diane française*, the last line reads:

   Ma Dame est France et moi non Lancelot

However, Jean Ristat insists that the correct word is 'son', and this is confirmed by Aragon (see *1*, X, pp.304, 404).

programme, for it begins by spelling out the aim of Resistance poets, viz:

> Trouver des mots à l'échelle du vent
> [...]
> Trouver des mots forts comme la folie   (*DF*, p.21)

As for escapist poets, they are charged with having turned their backs on man in his agony, and so, one day, they will blush with shame for having said, like Peter denying Christ, 'I know not the man'.

The last Resistance theme is the inspiration provided by love, and I shall deal with this aspect in the next chapter.

3. Themes

The two major themes of Aragon's wartime poems are love and France. As a rule, they are fused without artifice, largely because the poet's love for his wife strengthens his love for his country, and vice-versa. However, for the sake of clarity, each theme had better be examined separately.

(i) Love

Like all love poetry, Aragon's poems to and about Elsa express universal emotions which transcend time and place, much as they may have been caused, influenced or even determined by specific circumstances. But their chief originality lies in the way in which their author as well as his immediate numerous admirers saw them as contributing to the Resistance struggle. This is achieved in two ways.

First, the reassertion of the lasting character of love was seen — and was meant — as a challenge to the prevailing Nazi themes of blood, hatred, war and death. The preface to *Les Yeux d'Elsa* makes this point so clearly that one wonders to this day how it could have been allowed by the Vichy censorship: 'Tous ceux qui d'un même blasphème nient, et l'amour, et ce que j'aime, fussent-ils puissants à écraser la dernière étincelle de ce feu de France, j'élève devant eux ce petit livre de papier' (*YE*, p.32). The same idea occurs in a number of poems, though it is often, inevitably, hinted at rather than plainly stated. For example, even before he defied Vichy and the Germans, Aragon had, in the first part of *Le Crève-cœur*, shown his rejection of war-like mentality and his preference for a philosophy of life based on love. The message of 'Les Amants séparés' is not only the sadness of the lovers' separation (a hackneyed, though always moving theme) but the confidence that seemingly banal phrases of love are the 'aura' of 'un monde merveilleux' (*CC*, p.26).

A further example is provided by 'Ce que dit Elsa', whose theme is that a love poem, intensely personal though it is, and indeed because it is so personal, should appeal to thousands of others and bring them the comfort they badly need:

> Que ton poème soit dans les lieux sans amour
> Où l'on trime où l'on saigne où l'on crève de froid
> Comme un air murmuré qui rend les pieds moins
> lourds]
> (*YE*, p.104)

As a final example, let me mention 'Elsa au miroir', which describes Elsa combing her hair in front of her mirror, right in the midst of France's tragedy:

> C'était au beau milieu de notre tragédie (*DF*, p.31)

But she did not in the least forget the world of others, for it was the actors of the tragedy she was looking at as she was 'sitting at her memory':

> Et pendant un long jour assise à sa mémoire
> Elle voyait au loin mourir dans son miroir
>
> Un à un les acteurs de notre tragédie
> Et qui sont les meilleurs de ce monde maudit
> (*DF*, pp.31-32)

As for Aragon, he was looking at her both as a lover enjoying the sight of her golden hair and as a Resistance fighter grieving with her at the recollection of the martyr's death. So, quite naturally, he ends his poem, not on a purely personal note, but with a message of solidarity addressed to those who will set France ablaze:

> Et vous savez leurs noms sans que je les aie dits
> Et ce que signifient les flammes des longs soirs

Et ses cheveux dorés quand elle vient s'asseoir
Et peigner sans rien dire un reflet d'incendie
(*DF*, p.32)

The poet has transformed a fairly commonplace image (the loved woman's golden hair) into a symbol of fire, the fire of approaching liberation.

The second characteristic of Aragon's wartime love poetry which enabled it to become part of a whole people's struggle for physical and spiritual survival is that it stressed the impossibility of happy personal love in the midst of public misfortune. The poem which best illustrates this theme is 'Il n'y a pas d'amour heureux', of which the author gave the following interpretation during a radio interview:

C'est en 1943 que ce poème a été écrit. Ce qui est dit ici l'est sur le fond des malheurs de l'occupation. Comment aurait-il pu y avoir un amour heureux dans les conditions dramatiques de la France? Ce n'est pas là façon extérieure de parler, le poème même le dit:
Sa vie elle ressemble à ces soldats sans armes
Qu'on avait habillés pour un autre destin
A quoi peut leur servir de se lever matin
Eux qu'on retrouve au soir désœuvrés incertains
C'était écrit au temps même de la dissolution de l'armée française. (*20*, p.92)

The circumstances which gave rise to the poem constitute a striking confirmation of the relationship between public and private events. In 1943, Elsa suddenly informed her husband that she wanted to leave him, not because she had ceased to love him but because it was an accepted rule of the Resistance that man and wife, if both engaged in underground activity, ought not to live together so as to reduce the chances of being caught. Elsa wanted to be more active and so told Aragon that they should live apart. Although they eventually remained together and simply took extra care not to fall into the enemy's hands, the shock produced by the threat of separation was at the origin of the poem.

The opening lines have both an immediate and a long-term significance. On the one hand, they allude to the fact that the uprooting caused by underground militancy leads to the realisation that everything in life is precarious; more generally, they also make the point, further developed throughout the poem, that there is nothing human beings can take for granted:

> Rien n'est jamais acquis à l'homme Ni sa force
> Ni sa faiblesse ni son cœur [...]   (*DF*, p.29)

After drawing a direct comparison, in the second stanza, between man's unhappy life and the disbandment of the French army which was being carried out by the Vichy government under German orders, the poet begins his third stanza by suggesting that he is torn apart by his love for Elsa. But in the last two lines, we are told that the words he wove suddenly died away for the sake of Elsa's eyes,

> [...] les mots que j'ai tressés
> Et qui pour tes grands yeux tout aussitôt moururent
>   (*DF*, p.29)

This could be interpreted in two ways, either as meaning that the assertion, 'There is no such thing as happy love', cannot be maintained when looking at Elsa, or as suggesting that the poet's words are eclipsed by his wife's eyes. The fourth stanza takes us beyond the sorrow of a single individual. With the help of the idiomatic phrase, 'ce qu'il faut', which roughly means 'Think of all that's needed for...', Aragon reminds us of the price we have to pay for those brief moments of happiness, a song, a thrill, or a tune on the guitar. The last stanza repeats the general theme that there is no love without pain, but in the very last lines, Aragon appears to contradict the whole of his poem by asserting that the love between himself and Elsa *is* a happy one:

> *Il n'y a pas d'amour heureux*
> *Mais c'est notre amour à tous deux*   (*DF*, p.30)

This, I think, should be read as meaning that the 'happy' side of
genuine love stems from the joint awareness of public and
private suffering and the joint determination to overcome all
hardships together. Moreover, it is one of Aragon's beliefs that
all love is a mixture of heaven and hell, as he put it in his 1959
poem, *Elsa*:

> L'amour de toi qui te ressemble
> C'est l'enfer et le ciel mêlés   (*6*, p.46)

At this stage, the following question arises: in view of his
stress on the unbreakable link between love and sorrow, does
Aragon believe in happiness through love? It is difficult to
answer the question with an unqualified Yes or No, but I think
that by looking at his work as a whole, we can get a fairly good
idea of where he stands. First, he does not regard love as being
primarily a source of lulling comfort. To him, love is a turbulent
passion, not a soothing one. It can torment man and fill him
with jealousy, the latter being, as he once asserted, a form of
humility, a fear of being unworthy. On the other hand, Aragon
can also find solace in his wife's arms, and he often says so, very
simply and movingly. There is a contradiction between the two,
undoubtedly, but then as a dialectician, Aragon believes contra-
dictions to be the essence of life. It is not only in love but in all
other areas that there is an opposition as well as a fusion of
opposites, and, according to Hegel and Marx, it is this
opposition and this fusion which account for the very process of
being and change. Secondly, Aragon is more concerned with the
future than with the present, or rather with the present as it
paves the way for the future, and so the happiness in which he
has faith is 'cet immense bonheur posthume' (*5*, p.21), as he puts
it in *Le Roman inachevé*. Finally, Aragon does not believe that
genuine love is the selfish quest for happiness outside or against
the human community at large. He once told Hubert Juin that,
in his view, 'tous les hommes qui ont rêvé le bonheur des
hommes ont été amoureux' (*26*, p.249). And he justified this
assertion by pointing out that 'dans l'amour, chacun préfère à
soi-même l'autre. C'est là l'image tangible de l'anti-

individualisme' (ibid.). The same idea was conveyed in a 1959 article, significantly entitled 'Savoir aimer': 'L'amour, c'est d'abord sortir de soi-même' (*19*, p.128).

The main consequence of such an approach is that Aragon's love poems tell us as much about his own feelings as about the woman who is the recipient of those feelings, and it is this aspect which probably constitutes the salient difference between Aragon and other love poets. Before examining what he tells us about Elsa Triolet, it is important to be clear about what Elsa is not. She is definitely not a convenient symbol used by the poet when he wants to allude to France. As so many people, including some well-wishers, had (and perhaps still have) the mistaken idea that, during the war, 'Elsa' was an artful way of saying 'France', let Aragon answer them once and for all:

> les commentateurs n'ont pas cessé d'écrire qu'Elsa est un mythe, et que j'ai utilisé le mythe d'Elsa pour parler de la France en contrebande au temps de Vichy. Sans doute était-ce contrebande que de parler de la France, de son amour pour sa patrie, alors: mais mes gens n'avaient pas remarqué que j'en parlais en fait tout à fait ouvertement, et que quand je disais *la France, mon pays*, c'était de la France, de mon pays que je parlais. De même que quand je disais *Elsa, mon amour*,
> *Mon cher amour ma déchirure*
> *Je te porte dans moi comme un oiseau blessé ...*
> c'était d'Elsa que je parlais, qui n'est pas un mythe, je vous jure, d'Elsa, de mon amour, et je ne crois pas que j'avais à m'en excuser. [...] Bien sûr, que j'alliais alors ma femme et ma patrie dans ce que j'écrivais, [...] mais Elsa demeurait Elsa, et ses yeux, ses yeux. (*18*, p.351)

In the first collection, *Le Crève-cœur*, the picture we get of Elsa is somewhat vague, as the main aspect of her which is revealed is that she exerts a tremendous fascination on her husband and has transformed his life, but this by itself strongly suggests a powerful personality. A woman who was able to turn a 'mauvais jeune homme', as Aragon calls himself in 'Vingt ans après' (*CC*, p.12), into the kind of loving, compassionate person that he eventually became must have been a very unusual woman. The reason for the vagueness of her portrait in the early poems is probably that she was physically absent when Aragon was writing his pre-armistice poems, and that, in the immediate aftermath of defeat, he understandably concentrated on the stunning effect of recent historical events. All the same, *Le Crève-cœur* does provide some information about Elsa Triolet. For example, we learn from 'Les Amants séparés' that she wrote her husband a very sad letter,

> Une lettre triste à mourir   (*CC*, p.24)

At the time, this looked only as if she was reciprocating Aragon's sorrow at their separation, but there was one passage in the poem which alluded to the 'crimes' committed by unnamed forces of which Elsa must have spoken in her letter. In fact, thanks to Georges Sadoul, we now know that she guardedly informed Aragon that many Communists, some of whom were his personal friends, had just been arrested because of their public support for the Soviet-German non-aggression pact (see *25*, p.25). We thus get a picture of a woman who is not passively sitting at home, moaning and waiting, but of one who is rather very much in touch with contemporary events and acts as a messenger between the outside world and her husband. Another aspect of Elsa which is evident from the poems of *Le Crève-cœur* is her great beauty. One might say, with some justification, that all the poets who celebrated the woman they loved in their verse have gone out of their way to speak of her beauty. One would therefore hesitate to make much of the point that Aragon was no exception were it not for the fact that the mention of her physical attractiveness helps to remind us, as Aragon is so fond of stressing, that Elsa Triolet was a woman of flesh and blood. Moreover, the poet believes that physical beauty and spiritual qualities are inextricably linked, for the soul is reflected in the body, and vice-versa. Thus, in 'Pergame en France', he writes, 'Elle est si belle', and immediately afterwards:

Elle est la paix profonde et le profond délire
Tout ce qu'enfant naguère et qu'homme je voulais

(CC, p.30)

It is chiefly from *Les Yeux d'Elsa* that we get a much clearer picture. The opening poem deals exclusively with her eyes, because they embody the woman herself, a source of comfort to those who suffer, and a source of hope to those who fight. This is indeed the impression conveyed at the outset:

Tes yeux sont si profonds qu'en me penchant pour
boire]
J'ai vu tous les soleils y venir se mirer
S'y jeter à mourir tous les désespérés

(YE, p.33)

The poem then develops the idea that if Elsa's eyes perform the double function of reflecting hope (symbolised by 'all the suns') as well as despair, it is because Elsa as a person makes hope arise out of despair itself. This is achieved by blending the description of Elsa's eyes with images borrowed from nature. Thus, Elsa's eyes change when the weather changes, her blue eyes shine more vividly after they have been filled with tears just as the dawn is brighter immediately after the darkness, and when sorrow prevails it is her eyes again which perform the miracle of revealing that salvation is near. With this last image Aragon boldly compares Elsa to Mary, the Saviour's mother:

Tes yeux dans le malheur ouvrent la double brèche
Par où se reproduit le miracle des Rois
Lorsque le cœur battant ils virent tous les trois
Le manteau de Marie accroché dans la crèche

(YE, p.34)

At this stage, not only are Elsa's eyes loved by the poet because they are spiritually as well as physically beautiful, but because they are endowed with a mystical quality. This is but one instance of Aragon's use of religious imagery in his love poetry,

but it is neither a literary device nor an ideological compromise
on his part. For, although he 'worships' Elsa, he never forgets
her humanity; he rather suggests that man's natural yearning for
a being outside himself need not be seen in a theological sense as
his quest for salvation through God, but in a purely humanistic
sense as his need for other human beings, and, first of all, for
the woman he loves. It was only in 1963, in his long poem, *Le
Fou d'Elsa*, that Aragon fully expanded his views on what he
calls 'materialist mysticism', which consists in putting
'mysticism back on its feet', but the process of giving a
humanistic content to all 'myths' (not only in the field of love)
had already started in wartime. As he put it, 'Les mythes remis
sur leurs pieds ont force non seulement de faire rêver, mais de
faire agir' (*2*, p.95).

In the final poem of the collection, the title, 'Cantique à Elsa',
shows once more how Aragon makes a special use of religious
terminology, and the first line leaves no doubt that the 'hymn' is
addressed to an earthly, not a heavenly person:

> Je te touche et je vois ton corps et tu respires
>
> (*YE*, p.95)

Gradually, further details about the very real Elsa are provided.
In the second part, 'Les Belles' (*YE*, pp.97-99), Aragon imagines
her being greeted by other real women whom poets had
celebrated in their verse, first, Hélène (celebrated by Ronsard),
Laura (celebrated by Petrarch) and Elvire (celebrated by
Lamartine), and then Lili Brik, Elsa's own sister (a reminder
that Elsa is Russian, not French) and Mayakovsky's companion.
It was, incidentally, Elsa who first 'discovered' Mayakovsky and
who introduced him to Lili. She was distressed by the poet's
suicide in 1930, to which Aragon makes a discreet allusion when
he says (without naming him) that he died in the middle of
writing poetry, 'Mort un beau soir sur son poème' (*YE*, p.99),
and then goes on quickly to dismiss the subject for Elsa's sake,
'Mais ne reparlons plus de ce qui te chagrine' (*YE*, p.99).
However, the fact that he mentions it at all adds to our knowledge of Elsa as a woman who was responsive to great art and

who, before she met Aragon, had been deeply moved by Mayakovsky's poetry. In her own book on the Soviet poet, she recalled the impact he made on her when he was still unknown to the world and she was only a teenager.[2]

The fourth part of the poem (*YE*, pp.103-05) completes Elsa's portrait. The most salient characteristics which emerge are her simplicity and her dedication to other people. The simplicity is both a moral and a literary quality, for it stems both from her hatred of anything spurious and artificial and from her innate realism. What she says to Aragon is in character and not at all something imagined by the author. She frequently tried to check her husband's tendency to dwell in a world of his own where the ordinary cares of ordinary people are in danger of being forgotten, a tendency he inherited from his surrealist youth. (It is worth pointing out that Elsa merely tried to *check* this tendency, not to *stifle* it altogether, for that would have been tantamount to killing the poet's imagination, without which he would lose the power to raise us above the prosaic and the mundane whilst keeping his feet firmly on the ground.) Aragon reported later that when he read to Elsa the first part of his 1934 novel, *Les Cloches de Bâle*, her reaction was anything but enthusiastic. She felt that the novelist's lengthy description of Parisian high society (intended, it must be said, to show up its corruption) was much too restrictive, so she simply asked him 'Et tu vas continuer longtemps comme ça?', after which she added, 'Pourquoi écris-tu cela? Qui cela aidera-t-il?' (*19*, p.92)

Also in character is Elsa's plea that Aragon should think of others, not just of himself. It was indeed she, rather than abstract social and political theories, who helped to bring about his sense of commitment. In his 1965 novel, *La Mise à mort*, he recalls that he was 'bowled over' when his wife, affectionately called Fougère, first made him aware of the existence of others:

> c'est Fougère, c'est la voix de Fougère, [...] qui m'ont appris que je n'étais pas seul au monde, que le monde ce n'était pas moi [...] et comment voulez-vous que, de cette donnée étrange, *il existe d'autres que moi-même*, je n'aie

[2] See Elsa Triolet, *Maïakovski* (Paris, Editeurs Français Réunis, 1957), p.19.

pas été de fond en comble modifié, changé, bouleversé?
(*15*, p.18)

This brings us to the impact Elsa Triolet had on Aragon. Once
again, it is better to let him speak for himself:

l'amour d'Elsa m'a toujours apporté lumière, et connaissance de moi-même, et des conditions de la parole [...].
Elsa, tu m'as appris à demander mon chemin, à dire mon
désir, à proclamer le bien; et à chaque heure de notre vie,
chaque regard sur toi m'est encore enseignement, qui me
fait maître et de mon cœur et de toutes mes pensées, qui me
fait parler la langue des autres hommes. (*3*, pp.7-8)

This is no isolated statement in Aragon's writings, there are
hundreds like it, and some people might be tempted to exclaim
that he 'doth protest too much'. Maybe, but as far as I am
concerned, his words carry conviction, probably because I had
the privilege of meeting Elsa Triolet and of finding out for
myself what a remarkable woman she was. Be that as it may,
what matters more is the successful blending of personal lyricism
and social commitment in Aragon's wartime poetry, and this
would have been impossible without Elsa, irrespective of
whether the poet's praise of her is or is not excessive.

What is also achieved by Elsa's presence in Aragon's love
poems is the importance attached to *the couple*. The poet says
'we' as often as he says 'I', either in so many words or by
implication. For example, he writes 'Notre printemps c'est
d'être ensemble' (*CC*, p.38). He might have said, as so many
would have done, '*My* spring is to be with you', but he prefers to
emphasise that he and Elsa form a couple, '*Our* spring is to be
together'. His poetry is, as a rule, the poetry of togetherness,
and he claims that this is the chief originality of what he calls
'modern poetry':

Car il y a dans la poésie moderne cette nouveauté [...],
c'est que l'homme n'est plus pensé sans la femme, ni la
femme sans l'homme, et que la haute expression de

l'amour de ce temps, [...] ce n'est plus l'amant, mais le couple. (*17*, p.52)

This stress on the couple does not make love an impersonal affair. Far from it. For the couple does not kill the individual man or the individual woman, it rather gives each a chance to express his or her personality to the full. Aragon is no more eclipsed by Elsa than she is by him; they are both very much alive, with their own distinctive feelings, ideas and aims. One can really speak of a fusion in the best sense of the word, a fusion which preserves the identity of each element and yet transforms it. Not that conflicts never arose. The incident already related which led to the writing of 'Il n'y a pas d'amour heureux' is significant: Elsa and Louis did have disagreements, major ones even, but they resolved them together. Moreover, Aragon often had occasion to ridicule those who thought that he and Elsa formed a harmonious couple, free from prosaic rows or dramatic tensions. Such a couple, if it could ever exist, would be the last word in dullness, and, whatever faults may be laid at Aragon's door, dullness is certainly not one of them! When the critic, Jean Sur, wrote that the love between Louis and Elsa was never really 'threatened', Aragon exclaimed in a marginal comment:

> *Qu'est-ce qui permet de le dire? Pour autant que j'en puisse juger, tout amour est toujours menacé. Menacé par le temps, par le mal physique, par les malentendus, par les autres, par l'événement, l'absence, la misère. Et puis pour ce qui est de notre vie à nous deux, qu'en savez-vous? Rien n'est fragile comme ce lien de l'homme et de la femme. Il suffirait de si peu pour que cela se brise et qu'on en meure.* (*29*, pp.73-74)

He had already expressed his views on the precarious character of love in 'Les Yeux d'Elsa',

> O paradis cent fois retrouvé reperdu   (*YE*, p.34)

and in 'Il n'y a pas d'amour heureux',

> Et quand il croit serrer son bonheur il le broie
> (*DF*, p.29)

Neither would the poet claim that the Louis-Elsa couple is in any way *exemplary*. This would again suggest that he and his wife are not singular individuals, with all their idiosyncracies and particularities. For example, the fact that Elsa Triolet is Louis Aragon's wife is unusual enough, for married love is seldom the theme of love poetry, but it is not presented as a defence of matrimony. The only lesson it contains is one of partnership and everyday companionship. Gone is the uniqueness of lovers' meetings, the fleeting quality of their encounters, the treasuring of every moment spent together because it might not occur again. They are all replaced by living together, as most people know it. And it is not one of the least merits of Aragon's artistry to have endowed a prosaic reality with poetic beauty.

Finally, this insistence on the couple goes hand in hand with an attitude of deep respect for women, a respect which few male writers have equalled, because it neither idolises Woman by placing her on a pedestal nor considers, in Milton's famous saying, that man was made for God and woman 'for God in him'. Aragon's approach involves the recognition that woman has her own personality, and as such is man's equal partner, the equality and the partnership finding their highest expression in the couple. Although he had special reasons for emphasising these views in 1940-44, they went back a long way, at least to 1934, the year in which he ended his first realistic novel, *Les Cloches de Bâle*, with the pledge that he would in future sing 'a new romance', in which love is not sullied by the hierarchy of man over woman or by the 'sordid story' of dresses and kisses. In 1941, he felt the need to reassert his respect for women in order to protest against Marshal Pétain's proclaimed philosophy, according to which the woman's place was in the home, and against the Nazi view that the male alone was a conqueror, capable of displaying the 'virile' virtues of physical strength and endurance. In 'La Leçon de Ribérac' (*YE*, pp.115-39) his overt target could be neither Pétain nor the Nazis, so he chose to do battle with Henry de Montherlant, who had recently denounced what he called 'la morale de midinette', the ethic of the work-girl, and had put forward as an alternative to this allegedly 'effeminate' morality the fascist ideal of 'virile fraternity'. In opposition to this ideal, Aragon proposed what he was not ashamed of calling 'the cult of woman', and he linked this to an ethic which was steeped in French tradition, the ethic of courtly love. Far from making the believers in such an ethic 'soft', it rather demanded from them a high degree of courage, since the medieval knight was expected to perform many heroic deeds in order to 'win' his lady. And, taking advantage of the fact that the Vichy regime never tired of advocating a return to the past, Aragon concluded that *this* was the past which should inspire the French of today. He even quoted Gustave Cohen (a Catholic critic of Jewish extraction!) who had written that never had France been greater than in the days which gave birth to such unforgettable heroes and heroines as Arthur, Gawain, Isolde and Guinevere.

Aragon's 'cult of woman' is such an important aspect of his outlook on life that it does not merely go back to the pre-war period, but has been developed and extended in everything he wrote after 1945. His views on the subject reached a climax with *Le Fou d'Elsa*, in which he imagines, and at times identifies with, a fifteenth-century 'Mejnun' (Fool) in the then Moorish city of Granada who is madly in love with a modern woman, Elsa, four centuries before her birth. This allegory is used by the poet to express in the same breath his belief in love and in the future. For 'the times of Elsa' are 'the times of the couple', and, by paying homage to her instead of to Allah, the 'Mejnun' trans-cends the limitation of the present and divines that 'Woman is the future of man'. In 1964, Aragon told an interviewer that he visualised the society of the future as having a united couple as its basic social unit (*33*, p.135). This was not very different from what Elsa told Louis in 1942 when she suggested that their love ushered in a new world,

Tu me dis Notre amour s'il inaugure un monde
(YE, p.103)

(ii) *France*

At first, English readers might feel somewhat embarrassed by
Aragon's repeated declarations of love for France, as they
would by any vocal manifestation of patriotism. So, we
must start with what patriotism means to French people,
remembering that one of the chief differences between the two
countries is that we in England have not had to live with the
threat and reality of foreign invasion since 1066 — if one excepts
1805 and 1940, when Britain was threatened by Napoleon and
Hitler respectively, and when, incidentally, there was a
remarkable upsurge of genuine patriotism. France, on the other
hand, was occupied twice in the last hundred years or so, in 1871
and in 1940-44, to say nothing of the fact that it was on French
soil that the 1914-18 battles took place. Moreover, both during
the Franco-Prussian war and the Second World War, the fight
for national independence merged with the fight for social
justice, as in both cases the foreign foe, whether Prussian
imperialism or German Nazism, was politically and socially
'reactionary'. (The last word, a familiar one in French politics,
describes the attempt to put the clock back and halt social and
political progress of any kind.) The result was that even people
who, like the socialists, put social issues before national issues,
found themselves fighting the foreign occupiers in the name of
their socio-political ideals. In Aragon's case, it is significant that
most of his patriotic poems were written in wartime, when the
liberation of the national soil was the pre-condition for a return
to and a renewal of democracy.

The link between the social and purely national elements of
modern French patriotism goes back to 1792, when France
waged war against Europe with the double aim of preserving her
territorial integrity and safeguarding her revolution. However,
the link was broken in the 19th century, because, as France
became a big colonial power, patriotism often took the form of
aggressive nationalism and narrow-minded chauvinism. This

kind of 'patriotism' is alien to Aragon, and he writes at the beginning of *La Diane française* that its rejection by most people in the 20th century constituted a significant advance:

> il est indiscutable que c'est un grand progrès que de perdre ce sens de jalousie, cette haine du voisin, cet orgueil de son toit, un grand progrès sur les ténèbres, un grand progrès sur le néant. (*DF*, p.9)

Aragon's pride in his country is due to many factors, of which a crucial one is his belief that France's most important message to the world is the ideal of universal human brotherhood. He further believes that a fine expression of this ideal is found in the workers' anthem, *L'Internationale*, which was composed by a Frenchman, Eugène Pottier. In the poem, 'Ballade de celui qui chanta dans les supplices', he recalls that Gabriel Péri died singing the *Marseillaise* as well as the *Internationale*, and he calls the latter

> Une autre chanson française
> [...]
> Finissant la Marseillaise
> Pour toute l'humanité   (*DF*, p.39)

The French character of the song was so important to him that he lost patience with a number of German translators of his poem who had all omitted the word 'française' on the ground that it was impossible to find an adequate rhyme for it in German. He insisted that, in that case, they should have produced an unrhymed translation, and he added:

> Lier, [...] comme le fait même le montrait, le sentiment national et la solidarité prolétarienne, était un des buts de mon poème, et je pouvais difficilement supporter que, quelles que fussent leurs raisons de forme, des Allemands publiassent en 1945 ou 1946, sous ma signature, le poème avec une telle altération de sens. (*18*, p.325)

In view of this revealing incident, I feel it is right that a discussion of the national aspect of Aragon's Resistance poems should begin by stressing, paradoxically, their international character. For Aragon the two are not mutually exclusive, nor even radically different from each other, because, as we have just seen, he thinks (rightly or wrongly) that being open to other nations and their culture is an important ingredient of the French heritage. His own poems have been accurately described by his friend, Georges Sadoul, as 'un Chant du Monde' (*25*, p.49). The countries he most frequently mentions in his wartime poems are those he knows best and which he particularly likes, Spain, Italy, Russia, England and Germany. Spain is dear to him, partly because of the Spanish Republicans who stood up to Franco from 1936 to 1939, and partly because of her art (poetry, painting, music); Italy he likes for much the same reasons, as it is the land of anti-fascists such as Gramsci and Matteotti (see *DF*, pp.54-55) as well as the land of Dante and Michelangelo; Russia he has a double reason for cherishing, as Elsa's homeland, and as the country of the 1917 October Revolution; England he knows well and loves for having spent some time there before the war and above all because of her literature (there are many references to Shakespeare in the wartime poems, and to other English writers in the postwar works); finally Germany he cannot hate in spite of Hitler and the Nazis, for he remembers both her cultural past and her humiliating defeat in 1918. (Although the members of the French Resistance often attacked the 'Boches', to them the word meant both the German Nazis and their French collaborators.)

Naturally, the country which Aragon loves best of all is his own. He loves its land, its capital, its people, and the language he uses to say so is generally free from the bombast and rhetoric which are usually found in patriotic *speeches* (especially in France!). When he speaks of France, he tends to avoid obscure metaphors and sophisticated hyperboles, resorting instead to everyday words, those words which Elsa entreated him to use. For example, recalling his arrival in England from Dunkirk, he complains

> Terre Mais ce n'est pas la terre où tu naquis
>
> (*YE*, p.58)

Or, speaking of his gloom in September 1940, he explains how he understood its source on hearing someone sing an old French song:

> Mon amour j'étais dans tes bras
> Au dehors quelqu'un murmura
> Une vieille chanson de France
> Mon mal enfin s'est reconnu   (*CC*, p.53)

One can say that with lines such as these, Aragon's poetry borders on prose, but one should add that its evocative power is increased rather than lessened. As was frequently the case with Racine, it is the emotion which is poetic, not the words themselves. This can also be seen in those poems which are filled with the names of French towns, villages or provinces, as for instance 'Le Conscrit des cent villages' and 'Plus belle que les larmes'. What Racine achieved with the use of Greek names (e.g. the famous 'La fille de Minos et de Pasiphaé'), Aragon achieves with French names, as for example in the the second poem just mentioned,

> L'ombre de Jean Racine à la Ferté-Milon
>
> (*YE*, p.83)

or

> De Saint-Jean-du-Désert aux caves de Brantôme
> Du col de Roncevaux aux pentes du Vercors
>
> (*YE*, p.84)

or, in a broader sweep of the horizon,

> Le grand tournoi des noms de villes et provinces
> Jette un défi de fleurs à la comparaison
>
> (*YE*, p.84)

One place in particular is dear to Aragon, Paris. It is the city where he was born and spent his youth, and it breaks his heart to be away from it because it is occupied by foreign troops:

> Tendre Paris de ma jeunesse
> Adieu printemps du Quai-aux-Fleurs   (*CC*, p.50)

It is a city of great beauty, with a rich cultural past, and, above all, it symbolises the fight for freedom:

> Paris qui n'est Paris qu'arrachant ses pavés
>   (*YE*, p.85)

With what elation the poet greets the capital's liberation!

> Rien n'a l'éclat de Paris dans la poudre
> Rien n'est si pur que son front d'insurgé
> Rien n'est si fort ni le feu ni la foudre
> Que mon Paris défiant les dangers
> Rien n'est si beau que ce Paris que j'ai
>   (*DF*, p.77)

Aragon's love for Paris goes back to his surrealist days. In 1926, he had incurred the disapproval of most of his literary friends because he had written a novel, *Le Paysan de Paris*, (the surrealists tended to despise the novel as a genre) and had described in it, not an imaginary city, but a real one, the Paris he knew. In 1943, with no exacting friends to look over his shoulder, he felt free enough to make his 'Paris Peasant' sing again, and he truthfully says in 'Le Paysan de Paris chante':

> J'ai plus écrit de toi Paris que de moi-même (*2*, p.111)

As for the French people, what Aragon admires in them is their spirit of resistance, of course, but also their skill:

> De si loin qu'on s'en souvînt, il y avait des familles de
> pêcheurs, de chasseurs habiles à tirer au vol les plumes

dans le ciel et la bête des taillis débusquant, et des artisans
qui, de père en fils, se transmettaient les secrets du bois,
savaient courber le fer, tresser l'osier (*DF*, p.7)

and their tolerance in allowing believers and unbelievers to co-
exist side by side: 'et il y avait des églises et des gens qui n'y
allaient pas' (*DF*, p.7). These two qualities are expressed more
poetically in the last poem of *La Musée Grévin*:

Je vous salue ma France où les blés et les seigles
Mûrissent au soleil de la diversité

Je vous salue ma France où le peuple est habile
A ces travaux qui font les jours émerveillés

(*3*, p.75)

As in the case of his love for Elsa, Aragon uses the theme of
his love for France to contribute to the struggles of the
Resistance. He expresses his sorrow so that it can be shared, and
thus become more bearable, and his indignation so that it can
rouse his countrymen and stir them to action. Sorrow, as we
know, always goes with love, and this is as true for personal love
as for the love of one's land:

Il n'y a pas d'amour qui ne soit à douleur
[...]
Et pas plus que de toi l'amour de la patrie

(*DF*, p.30)

But such a painful reminder is not meant to discourage. Rather
the reverse; it is meant to act as an additional incentive leading
to militancy. The poem, 'La Délaissée', appeals to 'the memory
of tears':

Crois en la mémoire des larmes   (*DF*, p.47)

and another one, 'Les Roses de Noël', asks more pointedly:

> Le sang versé ne peut longtemps se taire
> Oublierez-vous d'où la récolte vint   (*DF*, p.58)

Like shared sorrow, shared indignation is meant to lead to deeds. First and foremost, the deeds of guerilla fighters, whose wrath should act as a spur:

> Entendez Francs-Tireurs de France
> L'appel de nos fils enfermés
> [...]
> Renaisse de votre colère
> Comme une voile dans le vent
> Vannant l'univers à son van
> La grande force populaire
> Unie et plus pure qu'avant   (*DF*, p.16)

Equally important is the contribution of poets, for theirs is the task of speaking for their land:

> Il faut une langue à la terre
> Des lèvres aux murs aux pavés
> Parlez parlez vous qui savez
> Spécialistes du mystère
> Le sang refuse de se taire   (*YE*, p.77)

Aragon's patriotic poetry, which gave 'a tongue to the land', is based on the concept of nation, not race. He stressed this in 1945 when he wrote 'La poésie d'un peuple n'est pas un héritage dans le sens racial du mot, mais dans le sens national du terme' (*3*, p.12). Race is a biological notion, whereas the nation is a historical and cultural reality. It does not depend on blood, but on a common territory, a common language, a common economy and a common culture. It is primarily with language and culture that Aragon is concerned. The first he describes as 'Un beau langage, qui servait à tout' (*DF*, p.9), and he does his best in his poems to use its rich vocabulary, everyday words as well as more outlandish ones, and to blend modern constructions with more archaic turns of phrase. With regard to culture, his aim is to make use of national traditions and national legends, by contrast with the Nazi myths of race. Hence his interest in the Middle Ages, a period he looks upon as important and topical. The importance stems from the fact that it was around the 12th century that a written French culture, as distinct from Latin culture, began to take shape, since some of the earliest French texts were called 'romans' precisely because they were written in the vernacular Romance language of Northern France at that time, Old French. Although it would be rash to say that the modern concept of nation was born as early as Aragon perhaps unwittingly suggests, it is a fact that a work such as the *Chanson de Roland* is teeming with references to 'la douce France'. Moreover, much as the idea of a nation was alien to the minds of feudal lords, towards the end of the medieval era it was slowly arising among the common people. In Bernard Shaw's *Saint Joan*, there is a revealing exchange between the squire, Robert de Baudricourt, and the peasant girl, Joan of Arc, the former saying, 'soldiers are subject to their feudal lord', and the latter replying that God 'gave us our countries and our languages and meant us to keep them'. As for the topicality of the medieval period in 1940-44, it was due to its exaltation of heroism, and Aragon felt justified in writing:

> Dirai-je qu'à fréquenter Cligès, Yvain, Lancelot, Perceval ou Tristan, il me semble bien moins m'écarter de mon temps [...] qu'à lire les ouvrages d'André Gide, de Drieu la Rochelle ou de Jean Giono? Sans doute de cet héroïsme d'aujourd'hui, de cette fidélité profonde, y a-t-il des milliers d'exemples vivants qui me dispenseraient de Perceval ou de Tristan. Mais en peut-on aujourd'hui parler? (*YE*, pp.137-38)

Aragon's love for France, like his love for Elsa, represents a negation of individualism. By this last word, we should understand, not the assertion of one's personality and the exploration of the self (Aragon is second to none in this respect), but the attempt to shut oneself off, to ignore others. In his youth, Aragon was tempted by this attitude, and he even wrote a sad

poem in which the line, 'Je n'aime pas les gens', recurred with
bitter frequency. But with the help of Elsa Triolet, he passed 'De
l'horizon d'un seul à l'horizon de tous', which was the phrase he
used to sum up the evolution of his friend, Paul Eluard. His own
wartime patriotism was his way of sharing his anguish and his
hopes with millions of others who were in the same predicament.
Such a sharing of emotions made him more himself, not less,
and this is why I cannot quite agree with Malcolm Cowley when
he writes that 'Aragon forgot himself in the struggle' (*23*, p.3).
Certainly, he was selfless and entirely dedicated to a cause
outside himself, but there was a dialectical relationship between
himself and his countrymen: what he gave to them, they gave
back to him, or, to put it differently, by forgetting *his self*, he
truly became *himself*. All the more so, perhaps, since his
patriotism involved drawing inspiration from his contemporaries as well as from the men and women who contributed to
making France's culture what it is and thus to the moulding of
Aragon's own personality. A man's personality is his own
distinctive characteristic, but it is largely made up of all kinds of
outside influences which the individual assimilates and
incorporates in himself. National culture is not the least of these
influences.

One last question remains: how genuine is Aragon's
patriotism? Both his political enemies on the right (e.g. Drieu la
Rochelle) and some of his former surrealist colleagues (e.g.
André Breton) charged him with insincerity, and both made
much of the fact that in the twenties Aragon had written some
pretty vitriolic stuff against France, the French army and so on.
They concluded that Aragon's patriotism in the forties was an
artificial pose, that it was a 'patriotisme de commande', i.e. that
he had been ordered by his party to parade his attachment to
France, the better to accredit the idea that Communists are not
the agents of a foreign power. Much of this criticism is dictated
by political and ideological passion, and we cannot here join in
the fray, either to defend or to attack Aragon. I thought it fair to
raise the issue, even though it cannot be solved in these pages,
and I would add that the real test is the poems themselves. It is
for each reader to decide whether they ring true or contrived. As

for Aragon, he never denied that he had changed (why shouldn't he?), and his answer to his critics, especially Drieu, he gave in the poem, 'Plus belle que les larmes':

> Vous pouvez condamner un poète au silence
> Et faire d'un oiseau du ciel un galérien
> Mais pour lui refuser le droit d'aimer la France
> Il vous faudrait savoir que vous n'y pouvez rien
>
> (*YE*, p.83)

(iii) *Secondary themes*

Among the secondary themes which occur in Aragon's Resistance poems, a frequent one is the poet's use of legends and historical events. The problem which is involved by such use is that of historical accuracy. In the case of legends, it hardly arises, as everyone is free to interpret them in his or her own way, provided that the liberties which have been taken with the generally accepted version are neither too confusing nor too obscure. With history, the issue cannot be avoided, and it would seem at first sight that Aragon treats historical facts in a very off-hand manner. This is not really the case, for he is usually the first to draw our attention to his distortions and to the reasons behind them (see *2*, pp.83-95). Moreover, he claims that there *is* such a thing as historical accuracy in poetry, only, in his opinion, it concerns the present rather than the past, by which he means that historical allusions, whether based on fact or on the author's free interpretation, should correspond to the mood of the moment, that they should be meaningful to the poet's contemporaries, for whom they are intended in the first place. He gives two interesting examples. The first one is the poem, 'Les Croisés', which deals with the love that the Crusaders had for Eleanor of Aquitaine, the beautiful queen who followed her husband to Syria, from where he launched his attack on the 'Infidels'. Towards the end, the poet confesses that he would rather not dwell on the unsuccessful medieval crusade, because it is another, more recent and more poignant defeat which fills his heart with grief:

Parce que j'ai le cœur plein d'une autre défaite
(CC, p.57)

And he transforms the Crusaders of old into modern crusaders, those who will soon arise to defend freedom:

Mais ce ne fut enfin que dans quelque Syrie
Qu'ils comprirent vraiment les vocables sonores
Et blessés à mourir surent qu'Eléonore
C'était ton nom Liberté Liberté chérie
(CC, p.57)

('Liberté Liberté chérie' is of course a defiant reference to the *Marseillaise* lines, 'Amour sacré de la patrie / Toi qui soutiens mon bras vengeur / Liberté, liberté chérie / Combats avec tes défenseurs'.) The whole poem was meant to lead to this conclusion, as Aragon explained:

tout le poème, écrit en 1940, au mois d'octobre, est évidemment mené pour la dernière strophe [...] qui correspond parfaitement aux sentiments des hommes de l'automne 40, qui n'étaient pas nourris de la main du maréchal Pétain. (*2*, pp.85-86)

In view of this, Aragon further explained, it did not really matter that he had made Peter the Hermit preach in the presence of Eleanor, when in fact it had been Saint Bernard, for, as he put it,

Pierre l'Ermite est le seul prêcheur de croisade universelle-ment connu, et [...] je vous demande un peu ce que cela fait qu'il s'agisse de la première ou de la deuxième croisade? puisqu'il ne s'agit pas du tout des croisades, ni de Pierre, ni de Bernard, ni d'Eléonore. (*2*, p.85)

The other example is the 'Plainte pour le quatrième centenaire d'un amour', which evokes the sixteenth-century poetess, Louise Labé, and her lover, the poet-diplomat, Olivier de Magny.

Aragon makes them meet in 1542, rather than 1556 as actually happened, so that the year of his poem should be the fourth centenary of their ill-fated encounter. This is because he has a special message to convey, that then as now,

> C'est toujours l'ombre et toujours la mal'heure
> Sur les chemins déserts où nous passons
> France et l'Amour les mêmes larmes pleurent
> Rien ne finit jamais par des chansons[3]

(YE, p.64)

Here is Aragon's justification for the liberties he took with history:

> En 1542, Olivier de Magny n'avait que douze ans. Un peu jeune pour l'ambassade et pour l'amour. Mais je n'avais pas le temps d'attendre 1956: c'est en 1942 que j'avais certaines choses à dire, fût-ce au prix d'une 'inexactitude' historique. (2, p.87)

The greatest liberty taken by Aragon, however, is not one that he mentions himself. It concerns the way in which he handles the Middle Ages. Not that there are many sins of commission in his presentation, but there are certainly sins of omission, for all the negative features of the period are deliberately left out to leave room only for individual bravery and respect for women, the two qualities which he wants to instil into his readers and hearers. The picture that emerges is not a complete travesty, but it is so one-sided that it becomes one which applies more to Aragon's imaginatively re-created Middle Ages than to the medieval period of history. Occasionally, the poet openly admits the discrepancy, but he dismisses it rather lightly, as he does in 'Pour un chant national', a poem which sets the medieval troubadour, Bertrand de Born, as an example to modern poets because he had not ignored the Crusades and their toll of

---

[3] The last line is obviously Aragon's reply to Beaumarchais's semi-serious assertion, at the end of *Le Mariage de Figaro*, that 'Tout finit par des chansons'.

suffering in his songs. Aragon writes that:

> [...] lorsque vint la grêle
> On entendit chanter Bertrand,

but he concedes in the next line that

> Le péril était différent   (*YE*, p.76)

Very different! The twelfth-century 'peril' had little to do with the threat of enslavement which faced France in 1941, and the Crusades were hardly wars of national liberation.

Consider also Aragon's presentation of Chrétien de Troyes's Perceval. In 'La Leçon de Ribérac', he recalls that the hero's mother tried to prevent him from having anything to do with war (which had killed both her husband and her elder son), but that he paid no heed to her entreaties. According to Chrétien, this was because war and fighting were in his blood, but according to Aragon, it was because he had decided to become a righter of wrongs, a 'justicier'. *That* Perceval, described also as 'l'incarnation la plus haute du Français, tel qu'on voudrait qu'il soit, tel qu'il est quand il est digne de ce nom' (*YE*, p.136), owes more to Aragon's (legitimate) wish to 'smuggle in' a topical message than to Chrétien's creation. He also bears a striking resemblance to Michel Vigaud, the hero of Elsa Triolet's 1943 novel, *Le Cheval blanc*, who dreams of emulating medieval knights in the twentieth century and rescuing damsels in distress as he rides his white charger.

Having said this, I must add that when Aragon deals with contemporary events, far from distorting them, he tries to be scrupulously accurate in every detail he mentions, relying in the first place on his own wartime experience. This can best be seen by comparing his treatment of the May-June 1940 events in the poem, 'Les Lilas et les roses', with his account of the same events in the novel, *Les Communistes*. The novel is especially relevant here because it is partly fictional (with regard to some of the characters) and partly historical (with regard to the political and military situation). Naturally, I am not suggesting that a comparison between the two texts, both written by the same author, constitutes, by itself, proof of historical accuracy. What

I hope to show is that the incidents mentioned in the poem are not symbolic or imaginary, but are based on facts as Aragon himself experienced them rather than on any poetic reconstruction or re-interpretation.[4]

In the second line of the poem, May 1940 is described as 'cloudless' ('Mai qui fut sans nuage', *CC*, p.40) in the literal and in the figurative sense. The novel confirms that 'Le ciel s'est dégagé, le premier vrai bleu de l'année par ici' (*13*, III, p.156), and gives many instances of the illusion then entertained that there was nothing to worry about (the figurative meaning of 'sans nuage') since victory was round the corner. The sixth line describes

Le cortège les cris la foule et le soleil

(*CC*, p.40)

and the novel gives such details as 'A Quiévrain, toute la population était là, du délire' (*13*, III, p.160). The seventh line reads:

Les chars chargés d'amour les dons de la Belgique

(*CC*, p.40)

and the novel expands:

Les chars, devant les ambulances, défilent. [...] Des filles folles se jettent contre ces énormes bêtes d'acier, des présents plein les bras (*13*, III, p.160)

and adds:

Mais les cigarettes, les bouteilles de bière ou de vin, les

[4] In order to get a complete picture of the period covered by Aragon, readers are advised to consult the following books. On the 'phoney war' and the defeat, one must mention: Marc Bloch, *L'Etrange Défaite* (Paris, Franc-Tireur, 1946; also available in English under the title of *Strange Defeat*, Oxford, University Press, 1949); F. Fonvielle-Alquier, *Les Français dans la drôle de guerre* (Paris, Laffont, 1971); and G. Rossi-Landi, *La Drôle de guerre* (Paris, A. Colin, 1971). With regard to the Resistance, the standard book is Henri Noguères, *Histoire de la Résistance en France*, 3 vols (Paris, Laffont, 1967-72).

fruits, les filles qui s'accrochent aux voitures pour embrasser les soldats, tout cela continue sous les *Vive la France*! (*13*, III, p.161)

The lilacs of the twelfth line,

> Entourés de lilas par un peuple grisé   (*CC*, p.40)

are also mentioned in the novel:

> les lilas ont fait leur apparition, tous les gens arrivent avec des brassées de lilas, la route en est jonchée, [...] les hommes dans les tourelles d'un instant à l'autre fleuris comme des dieux païens (*13*, III, p.161)

The novel also accounts for the Belgians' being 'un peuple grisé' by reporting their thoughts: 'ils se disent, bien sûr: voilà les Français! ils vont nous défendre, on continuera à aller au cinéma' (*13*, III, p.163). Finally, the June panic is described in the poem by such lines as

> Aux soldats qui passaient sur l'aile de la peur
> Aux vélos délirants aux canons ironiques
> Au pitoyable accoutrement des faux campeurs
> > > (*CC*, p.40)

and in the novel by remarks such as 'l'avance des meutes humaines [...] le bétail humain chassé par la peur' (*13*, IV, pp.355-56).

Equally accurate are the references to Aragon's own biography. The issue which these raise, however, is not one of accuracy, but one of taste. Opinions vary as to whether a poet should give many details about himself or whether his life and his thoughts should remain in the background since, as Pascal wrote, 'le moi est haïssable'. Aragon's spirited reply to Pascal is that 'tout dépend de *quel* moi il s'agit' (*18*, p.357). Without claiming to be in the least a model individual, he feels that he establishes a bond of kinship with his readers when he alludes to events in his life which might easily have been experienced by others, such as, for example, his first meeting with Elsa, or his anguish when he thought one night that she might die (see 'Un soir j'ai cru te perdre Elsa mon immortelle', *YE*, p.108), or his wartime experiences. He also feels that the unashamed display of his 'moi', doubts, limitations and all, might help people to learn from his past mistakes. In *Les Poètes*, written when he was in his sixties, he looks back upon his life and tells his generation:

> J'aurais tant voulu vous aider
> Vous qui semblez autres moi-même   (7, p.163)

and also

> Du moment que jusqu'au bout de lui-même le
>   chanteur a fait ce qu'il a pu]
> Qu'importe si chemin faisant vous allez
>   m'abandonner comme une hypothèse]
>   (7, p.213)

At times, it must be admitted, Aragon can be irritating, as for example when he expects everyone to share his likes and dislikes or to follow the occasionally tortuous meanders of his thought. But these, on the whole, are venial sins.

Lastly, one should briefly mention three themes which are closely related — the passage of time, old age and death. In the wartime poems, they are unobtrusive (whereas in the post-1956 poems they loom very large), partly because Aragon was then in his prime, and partly because he had other, more pressing worries. All the same, they do make their appearance from time to time. For example, the 'twenty years' *leitmotif* in *Le Crève-cœur* is not only a comment on the life of a generation, but on Aragon's own life which he feels has been somewhat wasted. It is with weariness, even a touch of bitterness, that he says that he will try and forget that he is over forty, as 'the waltz of the twenty-year olds' sweeps him along. The same weariness and subdued bitterness can be detected in this line from 'Il n'y a pas d'amour heureux':

Le temps d'apprendre à vivre il est déjà trop tard
                                    (*DF*, p.29)

The approach of old age is sadly evoked in the poem 'Imité de Camoëns', especially in the following lines:

Lorsque le temps s'enfuit pour ne plus retourner
Et s'il s'en retournait n'en reviendrait plus l'âge

Les ans accumulés vous disent bon voyage
Eux qui légèrement nous passent sous le nez
                                    (*YE*, p.88)

As for death, it is often mentioned, but it is not death from natural causes; it is death on the battlefield or under German firing squads. An early example of the former occurs in *Le Crève-cœur*, in the poem, 'Ombres', which was written after the bloody battles of May-June 1940:

Ils doutent de l'amour pour avoir vu la mort
                                    (*CC*, p.55)

The most striking example of the latter may be found in *La Diane française*, especially in the two poems which recall the shooting of Gabriel Péri by the Nazis:

D'une seconde rafale
Il a fallu l'achever   (*DF*, p.39)

and

Le souvenir a les yeux bleus
A qui mourut par violence   (*DF*, p.66)

4. *Poetic Technique*

It was 'right in the midst of tragedy' that Aragon wrote a number of essays, later added as prefaces and appendices to his collections of poems, in which he discussed poetic technique. He did so, not only, nor even primarily, because he wanted to foil the censorship and put forward his views on the content of poetry whilst pretending to analyse its form, but because he believed then, and has continued to believe, that the issue of form is of the utmost importance. 'L'histoire d'une poésie est l'histoire de sa technique', he wrote in the preface to *Les Yeux d'Elsa* (*YE*, p.13). According to him, concern with form is not the useless pastime of the devotees of art for art's sake, but something which stems from the wish to provide worthwhile ideas and deeply felt emotions with a fitting language, 'to make them sing', as he is fond of saying. In 1954, he rejected the view that debates about the technique of poetry were some kind of 'Byzantine affair', arguing that language is the poet's weapon: 'Les écrivains ont une arme qui est la langue, et les conditions de l'emploi de cette arme, les règles de son maniement sont d'une extrême importance pour l'utilisation de cette arme' (*19*, pp.189-90). How to make the best use of the 'weapon of language' became a paramount duty in 1940-44, when the poet was himself a fighter and when the word 'weapon' was hardly a metaphor. In the same way as the *maquisards* had to master the art of firing a gun or throwing a grenade, the members of the literary *maquis* owed it to the common cause to become masters in their own art. Aragon himself claimed that in writing his poems, he never left anything to chance:

> Pour moi, je n'écris jamais un poème qui ne soit la suite de réflexions portant sur chaque point de ce poème, et qui ne tienne compte de tous les poèmes que j'ai précédemment écrits, ni de tous les poèmes que j'ai précédemment lus.
>
> (*YE*, p.13)

Aragon further believes that the aim of rules is not to enslave the poet and clip the wings of his inspiration, but to make him truly free. He stresses in this respect that poetry which is genuinely free is not found only in what passes as 'free verse', but in the poetry which follows a certain pattern and obeys certain definite rules, both freely decided by the poet in the light of what he wants to say. This is why in his Resistance poems, Aragon deliberately makes use of some traditional devices in French prosody, hitherto spurned by the surrealists. He justifies his practice by claiming, first, that what seems to be a mere return to the past is in fact a novel form of invention: 'La liberté dont le nom fut usurpé par le vers libre reprend aujourd'hui ses droits, non dans le laisser-aller, mais dans le travail de l'invention' (*CC*, p.67). Secondly, he declares that his purpose is to provide an example of poetic freedom, including, when necessary, the rejection of the 'tyranny of free verse':

> Je n'ai jamais [...] voulu donner d'autre exemple que celui de la liberté dans l'écriture et par exemple de la liberté devant la tyrannie du vers libre, devenu à son tour sacré (*régulier*, comme on dit dans le milieu). (*2*, p.99)

In other words, for Aragon, freedom does not consist in the rejection of poetic traditions on principle, for that would be as restrictive a compulsion as the rule which confines poets to one given form for ever; real freedom is the refusal to be bound by any theories about form, no matter how 'free' and revolutionary they may sound, and the ability 'to say all', as Eluard put it in 'Pouvoir tout dire':

> Le tout est de tout dire et je manque de mots

Such an approach is reflected in the great variety of metres used by Aragon in his wartime poems. He contended later that this variety was by no means an entirely new phase in his poetic career:

> J'ai toute ma vie écrit des vers comptés ou non comptés,

comme je préfère à libres ou réguliers dire [...]. Ni *Le
Crève-cœur*, ni *Les Yeux d'Elsa* n'étaient des repentirs de
cette duplicité de mon humeur. (*2*, pp.99-100)

However, it cannot be denied that, unlike the surrealist poems,
the Resistance poems are seldom written in 'vers non comptés'
(with the exception of *Brocéliande*, where, according to Aragon,
'les deux systèmes alternent' in order to 'rendre manifeste ma
liberté de choisir ma prison', (*2*, p.100)) and that the poet
favours the alexandrine, the octosyllabic and the decasyllabic
lines. The reason is that these forms belong to an ancient French
tradition and so are best suited to the 'French' poems Aragon
wants to write in his German-occupied country. Moreover, as
they are familiar to most French people, they can help readers to
memorise the poems without having to keep them, a quality not
to be despised when Resistance poetry became illegal and one
could be arrested for having 'subversive' literature in one's
possession.

The alexandrine occupies a privileged place owing to the fact
that French poets have long regarded it as the best medium
through which to convey such powerful emotions as pity, anger
and admiration. As it was used extensively by both Classics and
Romantics, it represents a link with the country's literary past.
Thus, both form and content contribute to Aragon's national
aim, which is to remind the French of their own distinctive
culture that no invader can wipe out. But just as the Romantics
revolutionised the alexandrine by making it more flexible and
more in keeping with the different content it was meant to serve,
so Aragon's handling of the traditional line manages to give it a
modern look which is particularly suited to his contemporaries.
This modern look is the result of many factors, including
original rhyming schemes and images, which will be examined
presently, and purely metric devices, the most novel of which are
flexible verse breaks and frequent *enjambements*. The classical
alexandrine was made up of two equal halves or *hémistiches*,
neatly divided by a formal break or caesura which occurred after
the sixth syllable, and never in the middle of a word. The
rejection of this rigid rule, which had begun with Victor Hugo, is

clearly apparent in Aragon's poems. Consider, for example,
how a regular alexandrine is followed by a very 'erratic' one in:

> Reconnais-tu ce ciel / sans blé sur un sang brave
> La Marne / et vingt ans perdus / et les betteraves
> > (*CC*, p.22)

The scansion of the first line is a neat 6-6, whereas that of the
second one is 2-5-5. The contrast between the two lines reflects
the contrast between a public recollection and a more personal
one, the former being expressed by the regular style which befits
a solemn occasion, and the latter by the irregular jumbling
together of disparate images which erupt into the poet's mind at
the same time. Moreover, the five syllables devoted to the
beetroots make the reference to a trivial recollection even more
incongruous.

It would be wrong to think that the original way in which
Aragon discards the regular alexandrine amounts to a systematic
refusal to use it in its more traditional form. This is not the case.
For example, nearly the whole poem 'Les Yeux d'Elsa' is made
up of regular alexandrines. Here, as always, it is the content
which dictates the form: the use of Elsa's eyes to symbolise
tragedy and hope demands an elevated tone, almost a
declamatory one. Similarly, in the poem 'Du poète à son parti'
one can visualise Aragon on a public platform, extolling the
party which gave him back 'the colours of France'. Hence the
kind of eloquent (uncharitable critics might say 'grandiloquent')
style to suit the occasion.

With regard to *enjambements*, Aragon's chief originality
consists in making the sound itself, not just the meaning, carry
over from the end of one line to the beginning of another. In 'La
Rime en 1940', he draws attention to the following example:

> Ne parlez plus d'amour J'écoute mon cœur *battre*
> Il couvre les refrains sans fil qui l'ont grisé
> Ne parlez plus d'amour Que fait-elle là-*bas*
> *Tro*p proche et trop lointaine ô temps martyrisé
> > (*CC*, p.68)

Here, 'battre' rhymes with 'bas/Tr' of lines 3 and 4. Another example (not given by Aragon) occurs in these lines:

> Ah parlez-moi d'amour ondes petites *ondes*
> Le cœur dans l'ombre encore a ses chants et ses cris
> Ah parlez-moi d'amour voici les jours où *l'on*
> *D*oute où l'on redoute où l'on est seul on s'écrit
> Ah parlez-moi d'amour Les lettres que c'est *long*
> *De* ce bled à venir et retour de Paris
>
> (CC, p.20; my italics)

Here, in order to enable the first, third and fifth lines to rhyme, the sound of line three carries over to line four, 'l'on/D', and the sound of line five carries over to line six, 'long/De'.

The octosyllabic line occurs almost as frequently as the alexandrine. It is a form often found in French popular ballads, so it is hardly surprising that Aragon should use it for those of his poems which he calls 'songs'. Such, for example, are the 'Complainte pour l'orgue de la nouvelle barbarie', 'Pour un chant national' and 'Chanson du Franc-Tireur'. The first one tries to reproduce both the sound and the visual effects of a barrel organ: in each set of six lines, the fourth one is always a repetition of the second one in order to suggest the repetitive character of most barrel organ tunes, and the organ's rotation is conveyed by the way in which the lines are set out on the printed page, three lines starting from the left-hand margin, and three from the middle. In the second poem, each five-line stanza is followed by a long line in free verse which is printed in italics and is a kind of critical commentary of what Aragon considers to be the escapist character of Alain Borne's poetry. The last poem is a succession of quatrains, easy to memorise and easy to sing, as one would expect from a marching song.

Other forms used by Aragon are the decasyllabic, the heptasyllabic and the hexasyllabic lines and even, occasionally, free verse. The decasyllable, once described as the most French among traditional lines, is less solemn than the alexandrine. Its quicker rhythm enables Aragon to make ironical comments on the Vichy regime in 'Fêtes galantes' and 'Les Folies Giboulées';

to express his feelings more directly in 'Les Larmes se
ressemblent' (which evokes his naive ignorance at the end of the
First World War) and in 'Paris' (which tells of his personal
delight when the capital was freed); and to stir people to action
in 'Les Roses de Noël'. The seven-syllable line is used with
remarkable effect in 'La Rose et le réséda' and in 'Ballade de
celui qui chanta dans les supplices', both of which deal with the
ordeal and courage of Resistance martyrs in lines which have the
brevity of spoken language. The six-syllable line, which is in a
sense a half-alexandrine, expresses personal feelings in a homely
manner, as in 'J'attends sa lettre au crépuscule', or recalls
simple popular tunes, as in 'Elsa je t'aime'.

What is also noticeable is that a number of poems include a
mixture of metres. The poet himself gives the example of
'Plainte pour le grand descort de France', which is made up of
five-line stanzas, each one containing four alexandrines and one
hexasyllabic line. Other examples, among many, are the 'Chant
de la zone des étapes', in which each stanza has one octosyllabic
line, three alexandrines, and one final octosyllabic line; 'Contre
la poésie pure', in which each stanza starts with a decasyllabic
line, followed by three alexandrines, and ends with an octosyllabic line; and above all, 'Le Drôle de printemps', in which
the first stanza is made up of one alexandrine, one octosyllabic
line, one two-syllable line, and two octosyllabic lines; the poem
maintains metric variety throughout, and includes free verse at
the end.

An important feature of the rhythm of Aragon's poems is
their lack of punctuation. In this respect, the author shows
himself a disciple of Mallarmé, who initiated the trend against
punctuation, and, above all, of Apollinaire, who systematically
rejected it. However, whereas the poet of *Alcools* intended the
lack of punctuation to create some ambiguity, allowing for
different interpretations, Aragon justifies his own practice on
different grounds. His main reason is that each line of poetry
has its own rhythm which should not be broken artificially. He
defines verse as 'une discipline de la respiration dans la parole'
and claims that punctuation destroys 'l'unité de respiration qui
est le vers' (*20*, p.147). Perhaps one of the best ways of deciding

whether Aragon is successful or not in this respect is to take any one of his poems and ask oneself what it would gain or lose from the addition of punctuation marks. Let us, for example, try to punctuate the following quatrain:

> Etait-ce ici qu'ils ont vécu? Dans ce désert,
> Ni le lit de l'amour dans le logis mesquin,
> Ni l'ombre que berçait l'air du Petit Quinquin,
> Rien n'est à eux, ni le travail, ni la misère.
>
> (*CC*, p.42-43)

It becomes immediately obvious, first, that nothing has been gained, for it is practically impossible to read these lines aloud without resorting to the intonation and the pauses suggested by the question mark and the commas, even when they are not actually there, and secondly, that something might be lost as far as the continuity of the lines is concerned. This applies especially to the first line, in which the pause after 'vécu' should be hardly noticeable, so that the phrase, 'Dans ce désert', could become both the beginning of a long sentence (as suggested above) and the answer to the question, 'Did they really live here?' as if to say, 'What? In this desert?'. Here is just one more example:

> Ce n'est plus le temps de se taire
> Quand le ciel change ou va changer
> Ne me parlez plus du danger   (*DF*, p.16)

The advantage of the lines as they stand is that the middle one is both the continuation of the first one ('This is no time to be quiet when the sky changes or will change') and the beginning of the next one ('When the sky changes or will change, don't talk to me of danger'). Punctuation would force an artificial, unnecessary choice between the two.

Together with the variety of line-length, a great diversity of rhyming schemes is a striking feature of Aragon's poetry. His interest in rhyming is so great that he devotes two of his wartime essays to it, 'La Rime en 1940' and 'Sur une définition de la poésie', and discusses it at great length in the preface to *Les*

Yeux d'Elsa. His first reason for advocating rhymes is that they are particularly suited to French poetry. Historically, according to Aragon, rhyming was despised by Latin poets, but was brought to Gaul by 'le bas-peuple de Rome' and subsequently followed the fortunes of the French language itself (*YE*, pp.151-52). He therefore feels entitled to contend that it has become distinctively French. In other languages, such as English, for example, where the tonic accent does not invariably occur at the end of a sentence or word-unit, rhyming is less important and poetry can do without it. In French poetry, however, Aragon thinks that the rhyme helps to strengthen the music of the verse. He describes it as a great human invention, and, as he puts it, 'un dépassement de l'expression par soi-même' (*CC*, p.63). And yet, at one stage, it was poets themselves rather than the enemies of poetry who launched an attack on rhyming, starting with Verlaine's famous outburst, 'Ah! qui dira les torts de la rime?', with the result that modern poetry (but significantly not popular songs) has tended to turn its back on it. The main reason is that the French rhyme is fixed, whereas in other languages the stress is more flexible and thus new rhymes are always possible:

> La dégénérescence de la rime française vient de sa fixation, de ce que toutes les rimes sont connues ou passent pour être connues, et que nul n'en peut plus inventer de nouvelles, et que, par suite, rimer c'est toujours imiter ou plagier, reprendre l'écho affaibli de vers antérieurs. (*CC*, pp.64-65)

Apollinaire was the first poet who tried to overcome this difficulty when he abolished the traditional distinction between feminine and masculine rhymes. Before him, it was against the rules to allow a 'feminine' ending to rhyme with a 'masculine' one, even if they sounded alike. Apollinaire suggested that the new feminine rhymes should be those which have a sounded consonant, irrespective of spelling, and the new masculine rhymes, those with a vowel or a nasal. This new distinction opened up fresh rhyming possibilities, such as the rhyming of 'exil' with 'habile' (feminine) and of 'l'oie' with 'loi' (masculine).

However, Apollinaire's innovation did not really go beyond codifying the long-existing practice of popular songs (e.g. in 'La Chanson du Roi Renaud', 'gris' rhymes with 'écurie'), so that a more thorough rhyming revolution is needed. It is not true, Aragon asserts, that there are no new rhymes when we are in fact living in a new world. Who, he asks, has brought into poetry the language of the wireless and other technological inventions? There is a new world to explore, and it can be explored with the help of poetry, of 'cette méthode de connaissance qui s'appelle la poésie' (*CC*, p.67). The rhyme has a special role to play in this respect, because it is 'le chaînon qui lie les choses à la chanson, et qui fait que les choses chantent' (*CC*, p.67).

Aragon then suggests two new rhyming devices. One is the modern 'rime enjambée', also known as 'la rime Aragon', which allows, as we have seen, an *enjambement* of sounds; the other is the 'rime complexe', in which one word rhymes with several. The example given by Aragon is 'ivresse' rhyming with 'vivre est-ce' in 'La Valse des vingt ans'. Another example is the rhyming of 'diront-elles' with 'hirondelles' in the 'Complainte pour l'orgue de la nouvelle barbarie'. The simultaneous use of the 'rime enjambée moderne' and the 'rime complexe' makes it possible for all words to find room in poetry, even those 'qui sont avérés sonoriquement impairs et que jamais personne n'a jusqu'ici mariés à d'autres mots avec l'anneau de la rime' (*CC*, p.69).

Another reason for Aragon's interest in rhymes is that, according to him, they dispel the so-called 'mystery' of poetry. In *Poésie 41*, the poet, Joë Bousquet, had asserted that one proof of the mysterious character of poetry, of its defiance of reason, was that it used rhymes. Aragon's reply is that poetry is not at all mysterious, and his proof is precisely the existence of rhymes:

> Pour moi (et d'autres sans doute), la rime à chaque vers apporte un peu de jour, et non de nuit, sur la pensée: elle trace des chemins entre les mots, elle lie, associe les mots d'une façon indestructible, fait apercevoir entre eux une nécessité qui, loin de mettre la raison en déroute, donne à

l'esprit un plaisir, une satisfaction essentiellement
raisonnable. (*YE*, pp.150-51)

It is true that this defence of rhyming was published at a time
when Aragon used the medium of poetry as 'contrebande' in
order to 'smuggle in' ideas he would not have been allowed to
voice openly, and equally true that he was not exclusively concerned with issues of poetic technique when he wrote such
sentences as 'Une porte de plus à la rime, c'est une porte sur ce
qui ne se dit point' (*CC*, p.71). But it would be wrong to imagine
that once the need for veiled hints had gone thanks to the return
of normal conditions, Aragon had no further use for rhymes. In
fact, his post-war poetry continued to rely on them extensively,
which suggests that what he said about them in wartime was no
mere pretext. Moreover, when, in his wartime essays, he overtly
advocated taking full advantage of 'l'hermétisme de la poésie
contemporaine' (*YE*, p.121), he was reviving an ancient poetic
tradition that the times had rendered sharply topical, the
tradition of the medieval 'clus trover' or 'trobar clus', which was
also a kind of hermetic poetry, intelligible only to those in the
know, whereby the medieval bards sang of forbidden love
without appearing to mention it. Resorting to a modern 'clus
trover', which included, among other things, experimenting with
rhymes, was for Aragon and many Resistance poets another
instance of the fusion between form and content.

Whether Aragon's rhymes actually link the words he uses in
an 'indestructible way' and reveal a pleasurable, reasonable
'necessity' between them will naturally be a matter of personal
opinion. I think, however, that the following three examples,
one from each collection, might give some credence to his claim.
In 'Richard II Quarante', each five-line stanza has three lines
which end with the sound 'leur', a suitable echo of the word
'douleurs' that regularly occurs at the end. Sometimes, the
association with 'douleurs' is a natural one because the words
themselves convey sorrow, 'malheur', 'pleurs', 'pâleur'; at other
times, the association is one of contrast, as for example,
'couleurs' and 'Quai-aux-Fleurs' in the fourth stanza: both
words should normally be pleasant ones, but because the poet

laments the loss of the sky's colours and is saying farewell to one of the most delightful spots in Paris, they take on a sad character, which is well in keeping with 'douleurs'. As for the other two lines in each stanza, they are also linked by rhymes which either reinforce the similarity of meaning (e.g. the rebirth involved in 'renaisse' also applies to youth, 'jeunesse'; or the suffering of occupied 'France' is strengthened by the fact that it rhymes with 'souffrance') or produce an effect of contrast (e.g. the pleasing 'fontaines' cannot be enjoyed any longer since songs are put in 'quarantaine').

In 'Plus belle que les larmes', most of the rhymes manage to weave strong connections. Consider, for example, how in the first stanza, the rhyming of 'remords' with 'morts' suggests that people like Drieu are so full of remorse that they fear the re-awakening of the dead as a result of Aragon's harsh accusing verses; or in the fourth stanza, how the contrast between the rain and the blue sky is made more vivid by the rhyming of 'pleut' with 'ciel bleu'; or in the sixth stanza, how the image of a 'France' being reduced to 'silence' is more poignant through the rhyming of the two words concerned. Finally, in 'Marche française', some of the rhymes reinforce the associative effect of the words, for example, 'froid/croix', 'bagnes/Allemagne', 'envahi/haï', and 'nouveaux maîtres/traîtres', whereas others strengthen the opposition between them, as for example, 'se troublèrent/claires' and 'ciel clément/sans Allemand'.

A brief analysis of Aragon's poetic technique must include, in addition to his handling of metre and rhymes, some remarks about imagery, vocabulary and style. According to Aragon, poetic images provide a condensed view of reality, they are the 'short cuts' that lead to a more direct grasp of our own lives, our own selves and of the world around us. As he puts it, 'la poésie me fait atteindre plus directement la réalité par une sorte de raccourci où surprend la clairière découverte' (*17*, p.246). Moreover, an image does not merely reflect reality by condensing it, it rises above it, makes us visualise what our senses alone cannot grasp, and by appealing to our imagination, helps us to 'dream'. To the post-surrealist Aragon, this last word no longer means exclusively the activity of the sub-conscious when it is not controlled by logic and social pressures, but also, and according to him, more importantly, the ability to conjure up a vision of what is not, of what might be, without forgetting what is. A few examples will show how Aragon's images fulfil the double role of condensing reality and rising above it.

In 'La Valse des vingt ans', the image of the waltz is both realistic and imaginative. Its realism comes from the fact that the waltz is a dance performed by swinging round and round, which is in keeping with the poet's belief that the twenty-year-olds of today repeat the gestures of the twenty-year-olds of his own generation. Its evocative power is due to its association with happiness, so that the middle-aged Aragon is able to share the young's illusion that life is fun:

> Je veux croire avec eux que la vie est marrante
>
> *(CC*, p.28)

Both the music and the dance carry him away and he is able to forget 'his forty years in the year 1940'. In 'Tapisserie de la grande peur', the final line describes the hell-like reality of today (August 1940) by using the image of 'ce Breughel d'Enfer' and contrasts it with the hope of a better one suggested by the image of 'un Breughel de Velours'. The reference to two different painters of the same name (Breughel the Younger, known as 'Hell Breughel', and Breughel the Elder, known as 'Velvet Breughel') puts the whole thing in a nutshell, and in its brevity, is more telling than a lengthy description, followed by an equally lengthy expression of hope.

In 'Richard-Cœur-de-Lion', after proclaiming that composing a song is the one right no one can take away from him, the poet describes his 'chanson' as

> Blanche à la façon du pain d'autrefois
>
> *(YE*, p.74)

which is a realistic, down-to-earth reminder of the black bread which had to be eaten in wartime, and is also one way of voicing the hope that the days of white bread will return, especially as the song will be heard by everyone, 'et chacun l'entendra' (*YE*, p.74). In the same collection, the last line of 'Contre la poésie pure' asserts that Aragon has chosen blood in preference to incense, two images which sum up the reality of war and the Occupation, on the one hand, and the adulation of Pétain and the Nazis by the collaborators, on the other. But the poet is not just boasting of what he himself has done, for his images are so universal that they constitute an appeal to others to prefer denunciation to undignified acquiescence. In addition, the similarity of sounds in 'sang' and 'encens' further strengthens the opposition between the two attitudes.

Finally, let us look at two poems in *La Diane française*. In the first three stanzas of 'Les Roses de Noël', the images are extremely bitter in order to stress how the French were treated by the Nazis as soon as the Occupation began: they were like the wineglass overturned, or the ploughland upchurned, or the yellow trampled grass, they were exiles in their own country or beggars on their own highroads. But this was only one side of the coin; the other was that French partisans did not take the Germans' presence lying down, and in the following stanza, the poet likens them to the primroses that blossomed in winter and says that the gleam of swordblades was in their look. In the poem 'Paris', one line says that in the French city,

> L'air est alcool et le malheur courage
>
> (*DF*, p.77)

The image which equates the air with alcohol in a town which is fighting for its freedom makes us realise that in August 1944, Parisians got rid of all their inhibitions as they prepared to strike; the association of misfortune with courage suggests that the unbearable character of the one has led to the birth of the other. Another line declares that

> Rien n'est si grand qu'un linceul déchiré
>
> (*DF*, p.77)

The image of the torn shroud is a realistic description of the liberation which put an end to the Germans' killings, and an imaginative glimpse of the future which lies ahead now that death itself has been vanquished. Readers will certainly be able to find other examples for themselves. No doubt, they will also come across a few images which are trite and weak, but I think that the good images far outweigh the poor ones.

  Aragon's images are drawn from four main sources — history, nature, art and everyday life. The first one has already been discussed, but what needs to be added is that images from the past were particularly useful to Aragon, both in his 'legal' poems, where it would have been dangerous to refer to the present too obviously, and in his 'illegal' poems, in which today's trials and struggles were linked to those of yesterday. His favourite historical images tend to be those which rely on a well-known name, e.g. Joan of Arc, or a well-known battle, e.g. Valmy. Nature is represented in all its aspects, but chiefly by flowers and birds. The poet uses flowers in order to fix in his mind and ours some crucial historical events, as in 'Les Lilas et les roses', where the lilacs symbolise the illusion of victory, and the roses, the reality of defeat, or some abstract concepts, as in 'La Rose et le réséda', where the two flowers stand for communism and catholicism respectively. As for birds, it is part of a current poetic tradition to look upon them as images of freedom. Aragon is no exception, but what he stresses is, first, the Nazis' attempt to put birds in cages, and secondly, the futility of such an attempt, because, fowlers notwithstanding,

> Le passereau le merle et la mésange
> Le paon le rouge-gorge et le chardonneret
> Y donnent un concert [...]   (*YE*, p.79)

Nature is also represented by the human body, by the eyes, especially Elsa's which stand for most human emotions, by the heart, by blood, and so on. The two arts which provide most of the images are music, poetry's closest sister, and painting, which is itself the accomplished art of condensing reality into memorable images. Finally, modern images are drawn from science, as for example, astronomy in 'La Constellation', from technology, as the wireless in 'Petite suite sans fil', from aviation in the last stanza of 'La Constellation', and from everyday life, as in the reference to the black coffee which many French people drink first thing in the morning ('Un café noir au point du jour', *YE*, p.104).

Aragon's vocabulary is generally free from what Wordsworth pejoratively called 'poetic diction', for he, too, believes that poetry should speak 'the real language of men in a state of vivid sensation'. In the poem, 'Je ne connais pas cet homme', he sets himself the aim of speaking

> Avec des mots simples comme le monde
>
> (*DF*, p.22)

That he was not always successful we already know from Elsa's plea that he should be less esoteric, but on the whole, despite a few medievalisms, archaisms and outlandish expressions, the keynote is simplicity, especially in the last collection, in which the message is always plain. With regard to the puns which he is so fond of using, they do not seriously detract from the simplicity. Some of these puns are in fact quite successful in that they produce pleasing internal rhymes as in

> Tes yeux plus clairs que lui lorsqu'une larme y luit
>
> (*YE*, p.33)

or striking alliterations as in

> Absence abominable absinthe de la guerre
>
> (*CC*, p.16)

On the other hand, a few puns are quite gratuitous, and even ridiculous, as in

> [...] la radio
> Pleine des poux bruyants de l'époux qui se cache
>
> (*CC*, p.19)

(The 'époux' in question is Jupiter, hiding from his wife as he made love to Io.)

A few words about Aragon's poetic style. Like all poets, he does not mind breaking the rules of grammar, syntax, orthodox style and the like, and he even claims that the art of poetry consists in transforming such 'weaknesses' into beautiful things:

> l'art des vers est l'alchimie qui transforme en beautés les faiblesses du langage [...] Presque tous les poètes ont fait des vers admirables en transgressant les règles, parce qu'ils les transgressaient. (*YE*, p.17)

Here are just two examples of Aragon's own 'transgressions'. In 'Les Amants séparés', the poet asks his wife why her letter

> Fait-elle à la façon des cris
> Mal des cris que les vents calmèrent   (*CC*, p.25)

The poet has decided to split the expression 'faire mal' in order to give special emphasis to the second word. In 'La Rose et le réséda', Aragon compares the believer and the unbeliever when they are both thrown into jail, and he asks:

> Lequel préfèrent les rats   (*DF*, p.20)

This kind of interrogative construction is incorrect in French, and yet how dull the correct ones would have been (either 'Lequel est-ce que les rats préfèrent?' or 'Lequel les rats préfèrent-ils?')! That Aragon has his own distinctive style few people would deny, but he also admits that he frequently imitates other poets. In the preface to *Les Yeux d'Elsa*, he argues that all poets are guilty of this so-called 'crime', though not all would wish to admit it. In his opinion, imitation is really the tribute paid by one craftsman to other craftsmen who came before him. The important thing is not so much to use forms of expression which no one has used before, but rather to exploit other poets' gem-bearing seams in such a way that they truly become your own.

As well as imitating other poets, Aragon does not spurn his own past, and his Resistance poems, although they could not be described as surrealist, do retain some characteristics of surrealist poetry. In 1959, he pointed out the link between his former and his later manner, stating that 'il est indiscutable que mon langage ne serait pas ce qu'il est s'il n'était sorti du surréalisme' (*19*, p.89). For example, one feature which is common to his surrealist and his wartime poems is the spirit of revolt. Admittedly, in 1940-44, the revolt was mostly directed at political foes (but in their day the surrealists also attacked the 'bourgeois'), but its targets were also thoughtless convention, routine, smugness, all of which the 'angry young men' of the twenties heartily loathed. Moreover, the polemical style of the war period was the same polemical style which Aragon used in his youth. Compare, for example, the *tone* (not the content) of 'Plus belle que les larmes' with this outburst found in a 1928 poem:

> Je n'aime pas les gens
> Qui prétendent réglementer ma vie
> Mon temps mes goûts mes écarts de langage
>
> (*I*, IV, p.245)

Lastly, since surrealism passionately advocated poetic experimentation, the great variety of metric and other devices is also part of the surrealist heritage, as is the almost boyish enjoyment of juggling with words.

One final question: is Aragon obscure? Before attempting to answer this question, it is fair to point out that few poets have shown such willingness to reveal what he calls his 'secrets de fabrication' (*19*, p.45) in order to explain what he means and to show how he achieves his effects. (Readers will have noticed that it is Aragon himself who is most often quoted in these pages, rather than other critics, when explanations and illustrations are needed.) However, despite this commendable wish to lay his cards on the table, one must admit that there does remain a certain amount of obscurity. In some cases, as for example, in his earlier wartime poems, that was not his fault, as obscurity was the price he had to pay if he wanted to be heard at all. He even feared that he had not been obscure enough! For this is how he began the poem, 'Ce que dit Elsa':

> Tu me dis que ces vers sont obscurs et peut-être
> Qu'ils le sont moins pourtant que je ne l'ai voulu
>
> (*YE*, p.103)

The result is that quite a few of his allusions became clear only later, and often thanks to scholarly research and explanations by the poet's friends. In a number of other cases, it is Aragon himself who is to blame rather than external circumstances. For it looks as if two aspects of his personality served him rather badly. One is his powerful imagination, which leads him at times to resort to images that may be clear to him but cannot be so to his readers. To take but one example, why, in 'La Rose et le réséda', does the mignonette stand for catholicism? Not knowing the answer does not spoil our enjoyment of the poem, but it leaves us a little dissatisfied. The other characteristic is his encyclopaedic knowledge and erudition, which he parades so lavishly. Admittedly, this is not done to dazzle us (at least there is no evidence that this is the case), but it cannot be said that it makes him easy to read. One may note that this also applies to his predecessor, Apollinaire, whose great erudition is at times disconcerting.

5. Impact

Aragon was by no means the only Resistance poet. There were so many others, representing all shades of philosophical, political and literary viewpoints, and the demand for their works was so great that a number of observers in France and abroad spoke of an unprecedented poetic revival and praised what Pierre Seghers called 'l'honneur des poètes', a phrase which quickly became famous. André Gide commented in 1941 that it was from 'direct poetry' (as opposed to 'reflective poetry') that he was expecting a French cultural 'renaissance', 'from the mood that inspired Aragon to write the poems in *Heartbreak*' (quoted in *23*, p.6). In England, Cyril Connolly wrote that Aragon had managed to 'liberate in himself the music for which so many [were] waiting', and he expressed the wish that English poets might give us 'a music as lucid, as moving, and as largely conceived' (*22*, p.11). There were, however, a few discordant voices, which were raised both at the time and after the war, and they came from two different categories of critics. The first one, the collaborators, need not detain us very long, as they were obviously biased. It is interesting to note, though, that even they could not deny that Aragon and Eluard had great talent. One of them, writing anonymously, complained that there were many anti-German poems around, undoubtedly written by Aragon and Eluard, despite the use of pseudonyms, because, as he put it, 'il serait d'ailleurs très difficile, sinon impossible, de trouver dans Paris et en province même, des poètes amateurs capables d'écrire de si beaux morceaux' (quoted in *1*, X, p.17). The other category includes those who feared that poetry prostituted itself by serving a political cause, and some, like the former surrealist, Benjamin Péret, even spoke of 'le déshonneur des poètes'. Without going that far, Philip Toynbee criticised Aragon's marching songs by writing in the November 1944 issue of *Horizon*, 'I rate them low in literary importance because their spirit was primarily combative'.

Aragon and other Resistance poets replied to criticism of this kind in a collective article, 'Poésie et défense de l'homme', published in March 1944. They wrote in particular:

> Pour ridicule que cela puisse paraître ce que l'on n'admet pas c'est que la poésie puisse ne pas être insignifiante, ne pas s'en tenir aux amourettes, descriptions des beautés de la nature et autres gentillesses. (*1*, X, pp.15-16)

They further stressed that poetry is to be found, not in its subject matter, but 'dans le langage qui le crée', and quoted from the preface to a Swiss edition of Resistance poems:

> Ce n'est pas leur 'actualité' qui donne aux poèmes de ce recueil une valeur originale et neuve dans la poésie contemporaine. L'évidence seule de la réussite poétique a dicté notre choix. (*1*, X, p.16)

Whilst the reference to 'amourettes et autres gentillesses' is not a fair way of describing non-political poetry, I feel the authors have a point when they claim that poets have the right to deal with such serious subjects as war, national tragedy and injustice, and that their art does not necessarily suffer in the process. Otherwise, we would have to pronounce as 'unpoetic' such pieces as Agrippa d'Aubigné's *Les Tragiques*, Hugo's *Les Châtiments*, parts of Wordworth's *Prelude*, Shelley's *The Masque of Anarchy*, and Walt Whitman's *Drumtaps*. If we recognise that great poetry addresses itself to people's most fundamental concerns, there can be no 'no-go' areas for poetry. A poetry that seeks to remain 'pure' by ignoring all social and political issues is a poetry that ignores people. I believe T.S. Eliot was right when he wrote that 'pure poetry is a phantom' and that 'both in creation and enjoyment, much always enters which is from the point of view of "Art" irrelevant'.[5]

---

[5] *Selected Essays* (London, Faber, 1969), p.271. It is only fair to add that such a view is by no means universally accepted and that the notion of 'pure poetry' still

Another point which is worth making is that a poet does not lose his individuality when his voice becomes that of a whole people. First, because he himself is one of them. When Aragon repeatedly asserted, 'Je ne suis pas des leurs' (*CC*, p.17), he was not expressing an individualistic revolt against society as a whole, he was merely saying that he did not belong to the camp of the 'warmongers', precisely because he belonged to the much larger camp of people who yearned for peace and happiness. That his own feelings were those of millions, or so he thought, did not make them any the less personal and genuine. Secondly, there is a big difference between toeing a party line or writing to order and serving a cause in which the poet passionately believes. Whereas poetry that obeys religious, political or moral 'directives' is generally formal, unconvincing and stiff, poetry which stems straight from the poet's heart retains an unmistakable personal flavour, even when it illustrates a widely held attitude. Is Aragon necessarily less personal when he says, 'I love France' than when he says, 'I love Elsa'? Surely, here as in all other cases, our sole criterion should be 'l'évidence seule de la réussite poétique'. Malcolm Cowley believes that 'poets write best as lonely men, as rebels' (*23*, p.4; I am not sure I agree with his last point), but he is quick to add that Aragon and other Resistance poets could speak both as individuals and as representatives of their countrymen because most of France was made up of 'rebels' in those days. Individual rebellion merged with collective rebellion.

Whatever view one may have on this subject, it is a fact that Aragon's wartime poems had a great impact at the time and immediately after France's liberation, and not only among his political friends. For example, the Catholic, Gilbert Dru, who was shot by the Nazis, went to his death with a copy of *Brocéliande* in his pocket. There could not have been a more moving illustration of the fact that Aragon had spoken both for 'celui qui croyait au ciel' and 'celui qui n'y croyait pas'. Writing in 1965, Geoffrey Brereton commented that the Second World War 'was Aragon's greatest moment as a poet', but he went on

has vigorous defenders today, as for example D.J. Mossop, *Pure Poetry: Studies in French Poetic Theory and Practice 1746-1945* (Oxford, University Press, 1971).

to wonder whether his poems would last, 'now that the emotion of the moment has passed'.[6] On this issue of Aragon's impact in the future, not all of his admirers take the view that the whole of his wartime poetry will be acclaimed by posterity to the same extent. For example, Malcolm Cowley writes:

> I should judge that the future will prefer the 'legal' poems Aragon wrote in the first days of defeat. In them the need for speaking his mind without violating the rules of the Vichy censor was like a new difficulty, a new convention superimposed on the old poetic conventions. The devices he found for meeting it gave his poems of that period more depth, more richness, more density than he could achieve in ballads where his whole meaning had to be clear at a first glance. (*23*, p.16)

Personally, I think it is somewhat rash to forecast how posterity will judge this or that poem, as it will form its own opinion without bothering about what we thought. The only question which it is pertinent to ask is whether art which is firmly rooted in a given period is likely to retain its appeal. In the case of poetry, the precedents from the past, some of which I mentioned above, would suggest that it might. Sartre even believes that it is only when a writer 'embraces his time' that he can achieve immortality, because the most universal and lasting emotions, such as love, hatred, anger, can never be expressed in an abstract way and need instead to be embodied in creatures of flesh and blood, belonging to a given time and living in a given country. It is then that they can become 'eternal'. 'Eternelle [...] d'être datée' (*17*, p.25), writes Aragon about poetry inspired by topical events. It is very probable that in two or three centuries the French Resistance will mean little more than the medieval peasants' uprisings mean to us today. But so long as tragedy and injustice remain, so long are the poems which artistically reflected the tragedies and the injustices of 1940-44 likely to be remembered.

[6] Geoffrey Brereton, *A Short History of French Literature* (London, Pelican, 1965), pp.313-14.

In conclusion, Aragon's Resistance poems raise two questions which I should like to discuss briefly, the difference between poetry and prose, and the nature of poetry. The first issue arises because French poets discovered during the war that their medium 'had opportunities not granted to the others; that with its power of allusion, it could rouse emotions and lead towards courses of action scarcely to be hinted at in prose' (*23*, pp.4-5). Yet, Aragon, like Wordsworth before him, claims that there is no basic difference between poetry and prose. Why bother to write poetry in that case? Wordsworth's answer is that he wanted to 'superadd the charm' of 'metrical language'. Aragon is more specific. He believes that, although everything can be expressed in either prose or poetry, some thoughts really require what he calls 'l'aide nationale du vers' and that poetry is 'la pensée humaine portée au comble de son intensité', relying as it does, not only on the poet, but on 'toute l'expérience dans le langage de son peuple, tout le trésor des traditions nationales' (*19*, p.193). Of how his own wartime verse seems to support his point, I shall give but two examples. First, if one compares the following lines,

> Le malheur m'a pris à la Flandre
> Et m'étreint jusqu'au Roussillon   (*YE*, p.77)

with any prosaic rendering of the same idea, it will be readily conceded that without the imagery and the rhythm, little remains apart from the thought, moving enough as far as it goes, that misfortune prevails everywhere in France. Is this the same as making Flanders and Roussillon parts of Aragon himself? The other example illustrates the link between poetry and national idiom. The beautiful line,

> Ce qu'il faut de sanglots pour un air de guitare
> (*DF*, p.29)

owes its beauty, first, to the idiomatic, almost colloquial use of 'ce qu'il faut', and secondly, to its suggestive imagery, sobs for all our sorrows, and a tune on the guitar for all our joys.

What, then, is poetry? When he was asked that question, Dr Johnson replied, 'Why, Sir, it is much easier to say what it is not'. And, as a rule, poets themselves have wisely avoided committing themselves to a definition. Aragon has shown the same reticence, but on a number of occasions, he has drawn attention to some of poetry's distinctive features. Three of them are especially relevant to his Resistance poems. First, poetry is a form of song. As he put it in 1946, 'ce qui est proprement la poésie. Le chant' (*17*, p.10). He had, however, warned earlier that the word 'chant' had to be understood metaphorically: 'On dit chanson, on dit complainte, cela n'est après tout qu'une image, et qui n'est pas neuve' (*YE*, p.29). What matters is that poems and songs, distinct though they are, have a common source, the human need to express emotions rhythmically. Secondly, poetry tells the truth in its own special way, which Aragon does not shirk from calling a form of lying. 'La poésie', he writes, 'est l'art de mentir ou de dire ce qui n'est pas' (*3*, p.25). Interestingly, this is also his definition of the novel, for he asserts that 'l'art du roman, c'est de savoir mentir' (*19*, p.48). What he means by 'lying' is the writer's use of his imagination, but not with the purpose of deceiving the reader, the aim being rather to use imaginary facts or distorted facts to convey an important truth. Moreover, the poet or the novelist must learn the *art* of 'lying', for it is an art which, to use another of his favourite expressions, involves 'le mentir-vrai', i.e. 'lying' in accordance with reality and not in a purely fanciful way. Lastly, in *Les Poètes*, Aragon compares science and poetry, asserting that both provide knowledge, the former by testing hypotheses and the latter by using images. He calls the poet 'celui qui crée au moyen d'une hypothèse image' (*7*, p.194). Naturally, the knowledge supplied by the poem is not of the same kind as scientific knowledge, any more than it can replace it. With poetry, we get to know, not the objective world, but rather our subjective attitude to it. Enriched by this knowledge, we are better equipped to grapple with reality, and, when needed, to change it. That was the function he wanted his Resistance poems to perform. In addition, his poetry was meant to give aesthetic enjoyment both to the war generation, that had been deprived of nearly all other pleasures, and to later generations, whose understanding of past suffering and past heroism would be strengthened by art and its impact.

Select Bibliography

In the case of Aragon's works, only the most important have been listed. In the case of critical works on Aragon, only those which are especially relevant to the war period have been included. Unless otherwise stated, the place of publication is Paris.

EDITIONS

Le Crève-cœur, Gallimard, Coll. Métamorphoses, 1941 (reprinted 1946); Coll. Poésie, 1980
Les Yeux d'Elsa, Neuchâtel, Cahiers du Rhône, 1942
                 Seghers, 1966 (reprinted 1971)
La Diane française, Seghers, 1944 (reprinted 1945, 1965, 1971)
                 Bibliothèque Française, 1947

OTHER WORKS BY ARAGON

Poetry

1. *Œuvre poétique*, Livre Club Diderot, 1979 (Vols IX & X contain all the wartime poems as well as the prefaces and appendices)
2. *En étrange pays dans mon pays lui-même* (including the 1943 *En français dans le texte* and the 1942 *Brocéliande*), Seghers, 1971 (same volume as *La Diane française*)
3. *Le Musée Grévin*, Editeurs Français Réunis, 1943 (published clandestinely under the pseudonym of François La Colère; reprinted in 1946 with a preface, 'Les Poissons noirs')
4. *Les Yeux et la mémoire*, Gallimard, 1954
5. *Le Roman inachevé*, Gallimard, 1956
6. *Elsa*, Gallimard, 1959
7. *Les Poètes*, Gallimard, 1960
8. *Le Fou d'Elsa*, Gallimard, 1963

Novels

9. *Les Cloches de Bâle*, Denoël et Steele, 1934 (Livre de Poche, 1954; Gallimard, Coll. Folio, 1972)
10. *Les Beaux Quartiers*, Denoël et Steele, 1936 (Livre de Poche, 1936; Gallimard, Coll. Folio, 1972)
11. *Les Voyageurs de l'impériale*, Gallimard, 1943 (truncated, not acknowledged by the author). Gallimard, Coll. Blanche,1947; Coll. Folio, 1972 (Livre de Poche, 1961)

12. *Aurélien*, Gallimard, Coll. Blanche, 1944; Coll. Folio, 1976 (Livre de Poche, 1964)
13. *Les Communistes*, Bibliothèque française, 1949-51 (6 vols); Editeurs Français Réunis, 1966 (4 vols, rewritten and revised by the author; edition used in this study)
14. *La Semaine sainte*, Gallimard, 1958
15. *La Mise à mort*, Gallimard, Coll. Blanche, 1965; Coll. Folio, 1973
16. *Blanche ou l'oubli*, Gallimard, Coll. Blanche, 1967; Coll. Folio, 1972

Note also that all the novels are included in the *Œuvres romanesques croisées (d'Elsa Triolet et d'Aragon)*, Robert Laffont, 1964-74 (42 vols)

Critical works
17. *Chroniques du bel canto*, Geneva, Skira, 1947
18. *Littératures soviétiques*, Denoël, 1955
19. *J'abats mon jeu*, Editeurs Français Réunis, 1959

Interviews
20. *Entretiens avec Francis Crémieux*, Gallimard, 1964
21. *Aragon parle avec Dominique Arban*, Seghers, 1968

WORKS ON ARAGON

Introductions and prefaces to anthologies
22. André Labarthe & Cyril Connolly, Preface (in French) and Introduction (in English) to *Le Crève-cœur et Les Yeux d'Elsa*, London, La France Libre, 1944
23. Malcolm Cowley, 'Poet of this war', Introduction to *Aragon, Poet of Resurgent France* (anthology in English), London, Pilot Press, 1946
24. Claude Roy, *Aragon*, Seghers, 1945
25. Georges Sadoul, *Aragon*, Seghers, 1967

Books on Aragon
26. Hubert Juin, *Aragon*, Gallimard, 1960
27. Roger Garaudy, *L'Itinéraire d'Aragon*, Gallimard, 1961
28. Georges Raillard, *Aragon*, Editions Universitaires, 1964
29. Jean Sur, *Aragon, le réalisme de l'amour* (with marginal comments by Aragon), Le Centurion, 1966
30. Bernard Lecherbonnier, *Aragon*, Bordas, 1971
31. Bernard Lecherbonnier (ed.), *Les Critiques de notre temps et Aragon*, Garnier, 1976

Books on specific aspects
32. Suzanne Labry, *Aragon, poète d'Elsa*, C.E.R.M., 1965
33. Charles Haroche, *L'Idée de l'amour dans 'Le Fou d'Elsa' et l'œuvre d'Aragon*, Gallimard, 1966

General works

34. M. Adereth, *Commitment in Modern French Literature*, London, Gollancz, 1967
35. R.M. Albérès, *La Révolte des écrivains d'aujourd'hui*, Corrêa, 1949
36. André Rousseaux, *Littérature du XXe siècle* (vol. III), Albin Michel, 1949

Details of first publication of individual poems

37. Crispin Geoghegan, *Louis Aragon: essai de bibliographie* (vol. I, 1918-1959), London, Grant & Cutler, 1979

CRITICAL GUIDES TO FRENCH TEXTS

edited by
Roger Little, Wolfgang van Emden, David Williams

1. **David Bellos.** Balzac: La Cousine Bette
2. **Rosemarie Jones.** Camus: L'Etranger *and* La Chute
3. **W.D. Redfern.** Queneau: Zazie dans le métro
4. **R.C. Knight.** Corneille: Horace
5. **Christopher Todd.** Voltaire: Dictionnaire philosophique
6. **J.P. Little.** Beckett: En attendant Godot *and* Fin de partie
7. **Donald Adamson.** Balzac: Illusions perdues
8. **David Coward.** Duras: Moderato cantabile
9. **Michael Tilby.** Gide: Les Faux-Monnayeurs
10. **Vivienne Mylne.** Diderot: La Religieuse
11. **Elizabeth Fallaize.** Malraux: La Voie royale
12. **H.T. Barnwell.** Molière: Le Malade imaginaire
13. **Graham E. Rodmell.** Marivaux: Le Jeu de l'amour et du hasard *and* Les Fausses Confidences
14. **Keith Wren.** Hugo: Hernani *and* Ruy Blas
15. **Peter S. Noble.** Beroul's Tristan *and the* Folie de Berne
16. **Paula Clifford.** Marie de France: Lais
17. **David Coward.** Marivaux: La Vie de Marianne *and* Le Paysan parvenu
18. **J.H. Broome.** Molière: L'Ecole des femmes *and* Le Misanthrope
19. **B.G. Garnham.** Robbe-Grillet: Les Gommes *and* Le Voyeur
20. **J.P. Short.** Racine: Phèdre
21. **Robert Niklaus.** Beaumarchais: Le Mariage de Figaro
22. **Anthony Cheal Pugh.** Simon: Histoire
23. **Lucie Polak.** Chrétien de Troyes: Cligés
24. **John Cruickshank.** Pascal: Pensées
25. **Ceri Crossley.** Musset: Lorenzaccio
26. **J.W. Scott.** Madame de Lafayette: La Princesse de Clèves
27. **John Holyoake.** Montaigne: Essais
28. **Peter Jimack.** Rousseau: Emile
29. **Roger Little.** Rimbaud: Illuminations
30. **Barbara Wright and David Scott.** Baudelaire: La Fanfarlo *and* Le Spleen de Paris